S0-BXM-341

This book is a collaborative effort. Writers from all over the world submitted their work for consideration, with 59 stories making the final cut. All contributors are compensated for their stories.

Publishing Syndicate strongly encourages you to submit your story for one of its many upcoming anthologies.

For information on how to submit your story, go to www.PublishingSyndicate.com.

Dedication

To my favorite past employers, who taught me so much: Amy Hartshorn of Hart C's Restaurant; Eugene J. (Gene) Carlson and Ella Barber of IPCO Federal Credit Union and Bob Nelson, who operated retail and wholesale businesses. I gained knowledge on each job that made me a better employee on the next.

Amy taught me to cook a darned good steakburger and also taught me the importance of good customer service. Gene and Ella taught me about cash handling, accuracy, marketing and more customer service. And when I worked for Bob, whom I later married, I was able to use all of the skills I had learned on earlier jobs, including occasionally cooking a darned good steakburger.

I wouldn't be who I am today without these great mentors. Thank you.

~~ Pat Nelson

My husband Bob at his store Bird Boys. I was mentored by a bird brain. That explains a lot!

CONTENTS

3 Human Resources

4 Open Mouth

5 I Am Woman

Acknowledgments

Thank you all for your hard work!

From Pat

To my husband, Bob, for his support. After working together for nearly 30 years in various retail and wholesale businesses, I appreciate Bob encouraging me to take a step away from our businesses to pursue my passion of writing and editing. I also appreciate his help in setting up and tearing down my booths at book fairs. It's a lot of work, and I couldn't do it without his great ideas and assistance. If I had to do it alone, I'd probably just have an overturned bucket to sit on and a rickety card table to hold my books.

I owe thanks, too, to my granddaughter Chelsea Rose and to my friend Nona Perry, who have both volunteered many hours to assist me at book fairs and readings. I count on Chelsea to operate the Square credit card reader for me because, at age 14, she is much smarter than her grandma!

From Dahlynn and Ken

Thank you to Dahlynn's teenage son Shawn. Our family has survived the creation of yet another book, and your help, patience and support was key to that success. We love you!

And from all of us at Publishing Syndicate

A special thanks to the many writers who submitted stories for this book. Without you, this book would not have come together like it did. Your stories are wonderful and we thank you for sharing them with us and the world. We only wish we could have printed every story submitted.

Keep those stories coming in for future NYMB titles: www.PublishingSyndicate.com.

Introduction

"Your work is going to fill a large part of your life, and the only way to be truly satisfied is to do what you believe is great work. And the only way to do great work is to love what you do. If you haven't found it yet, keep looking. Don't settle."

~ ~ *Steve Jobs*

When I graduated from high school, people asked, "What are you going to be?"

Be? I scoured the college catalog. If I were to take a two-year nursing program, I could be a nurse.

Happy to have an answer, I signed up for the nursing program where I quickly made new friends. One day, the instructor announced, "Tomorrow we will learn to give enemas." *Will we have to practice on each other?* I worried. I couldn't think of a better way to lose friends, so I never went back. Read more humorous workplace stories in the chapter *Out to Lunch and Paying the Price.*

Many of us end up on jobs that we either love or hate. I worked for a credit union for several years. I loved just about everything about that job. My male boss complimented me one day, saying, "I wish I could find a man with your capabilities." I was so proud, not knowing enough to be insulted . . . that was before women's lib! Read stories about women in the workplace in the chapter *I Am Woman, Watch Me Soar.*

Eventually, I left the credit union and bought a restaurant, the one mentioned in my story "Antacids on the Menu." I only hated that job for four of the five years I owned the place. I gained a great respect for people in business and I vowed to never again own my own business. If you own a business, I'm sure you, too, have stories—some good, some bad. Can you now laugh at some of the horror stories? I hope you're one of the lucky ones with a success story.

Next, I was hired to do bookkeeping and marketing for a man named "Bob" at his discount variety store. Ten years later, I married Bob, which meant that I was again a business owner. Along with our success stories, we've had enough horror stories to fill several books. Working with a spouse or other family members can create additional problems or opportunities, as you will read in the chapter *Human Resources, Relationships in the Workplace*.

Now, a couple years beyond when I had expected to retire, I'm busy with another career. I write and edit, and I co-create *Not Your Mother's Books*. I plan to continue this career for as many years as I am able. Finally, I know what I want to be—a writer.

Enjoy the stories in this book and revisit your own humorous stories of working for a living. And if you still haven't found your dream job, keep looking. Don't settle.

~~ Pat Nelson

CHAPTER ONE

Out to Lunch . . .

_____

. . . and paying the price!

_____

Crop Circles

by
Debra Ayers Brown

The alarm screamed, and I bolted out of bed. But there was one problem. The alarm clock remained set on weekend alarm time. I was two hours behind on a Monday morning when I had an important presentation scheduled.

"Why today?" I said aloud to no one, cursing the fact I had no time to shower. No time to wash my hair. All on a day when I wanted to look my best.

Fortunately, I had packed my briefcase and laid out my clothes the night before. So I sponged off, slathered on deodorant and scrambled into my professional attire. At the last moment, I grabbed the dry shampoo, slung my head over and sprayed it in circles. I flipped my hair back, combed it and headed for the door. When I arrived at my meeting destination, I refreshed my lipstick and powdered my nose, careful to be well-groomed for my part of the program.

Everything went well during the talk on professional

branding. I moved from the podium and worked the audience, trying to engage instead of just giving information. As I critiqued several online business sites, I said to the attendees, "Consistency is critical for your image—offline and online. If not, there's a disconnect."

One after another nodded in agreement, smiling. My energy level kicked up a notch as I continued. We explored developing their messages and discussed the importance of authenticity. Everyone seemed interested in learning more. They even laughed at the cartoons on the screen that I had sprinkled throughout the presentation. A hushed murmur moved through the crowd as I completed the last part of the Power Point presentation on a high.

I stayed afterward, talking to members of the audience. Everyone seemed to be in a great mood. I lingered, caught up in the afterglow of a successful morning.

It wasn't until I returned home that my mood changed.

"What's wrong with your hair?" my daughter Meredith asked with a cocked brow.

"What do you mean?" I reached up to smooth any stray strands.

"I don't know what you did to it, but your hair is black in the back." She giggled. "Kind of."

"Kind of?"

"There are black circles," Meredith answered, shrugging.

I rushed to the bathroom with Meredith following close behind, laughing.

I grabbed a hand mirror and gasped. It looked like I'd spray-painted black circles on my hair. The black stood out against my light hair like a zebra's behind in the sunshine.

"Well?" Meredith stared at me. "What'd you do to it?"

"I can't imagine," I mumbled, still twisting and turning, trying to get a better look.

"Oh," Meredith said with a laugh. "I see what happened." She picked up the container of dry shampoo and pointed to the label. "This is made for dark hair."

I looked closer at the label. *Brunette.* I had no idea they made dry shampoo for different hair colors.

As I stared at my reflection, my presentation flashed before my eyes. I thought the audience had been responding to my content and laughing at the cartoons I'd used throughout my talk. Now I knew better.

"I probably didn't do much for my own branding today," I said to my daughter. "Maybe next time, I'll stick red-hot metal against my hindquarters to demonstrate what can happen if you make a misstep."

"That'd be less embarrassing," Meredith agreed, giggling. "But what if someone shared your crop circles on all the social media outlets?"

Oh. God. No. Panicked thoughts raced through my mind, all in black-and-white craziness. *Am I already trending from the morning's spectacle?* I remembered the cellphone flashes during my presentation. *Are there Facebook posts of my two-toned hair? Tweets about Cruella de Vil with 101 Dalmatians curled up in my hair? A YouTube video branding me as the skunk of my profession? Would the unwanted attention be all bad?*

Like every good PR professional, my thoughts turned to

prime time. But I decided a viral sensation about a marketing pro's mishaps while teaching a branding class wouldn't be the break I'd want. No matter. My desire to keep my debacle offline wouldn't stop *Entertainment Tonight* from featuring the video with the headline, "Branding expert decides to check out the theory that no publicity is bad publicity." Fallon would tease his show with, "Crop circles mysteriously appeared in Georgia when branding expert . . . " And all the news stations would latch on to the story, "Marketing expert shows what *not* to do when addressing a crowd."

Meredith stared at me while I ran my fingers through my hair. "Well, you're the one they call when there's a crisis," she said. "How would you spin this situation for someone else?"

"I'd tell them not to worry about it and to laugh when others mentioned it," I answered. I knew my stuff. "And they'd probably be top of mind when someone thought of branding or dry shampoo or crop circles. How could that be a bad thing?"

My fiasco turned out fine. No Facebook posts. No Tweets. No YouTube videos.

With my confidence restored, I remembered I had worked hard to transform from traditional marketing into social selling. It wasn't an overnight phenomenon. The strategies I'd developed worked. One morning fiasco wouldn't derail my efforts. I had the goods to propel my career into a viral sensation—with or without crop circles.

Pole Dancing or Peach Cobbler?

by
Jim Tobalski

Over the span of my 37-year management career, my biggest hiring challenge occurred in the 1990s when my department added a secretarial position. The search for our new assistant started with excellent preliminary results. Human resources recruited several good candidates whom my staff narrowed down to a pair of finalists. Now it was my turn for discernment and selection.

I reviewed the first resume, jam-packed with experience, accolades, high performance and prestigious employers. The candidate appeared to be in her 50s, about 20 years my senior. This created the perfect age gap, a relationship between subordinate and supervisor of almost motherly potential: Fresh pie every morning. Meticulous screening of phone calls. Darning my argyle socks. Routine purging of old cabinet files. Nonsexual shoulder massages after marathon budget meetings. *Sweet!* I thought.

The second resume contained similar but not identical assets. This applicant appeared about 10 years my junior. She had completed impressive academic training and was proficient in a variety of computer programs. In addition, she demonstrated some out-of-the-box thinking by designing her curriculum vitae to resemble pages from *Time* magazine. *What a go-getter!*

Of course, both candidates demanded fair consideration, so I carefully reviewed their work histories provided by the recruiter. After a few yawns and head scratches, I stumbled upon a small detail from the page of the younger applicant, something I hastily overlooked during the initial frenzy that so often accompanies flipping through resumes. There, listed under "current employer," were two companies: 1) a well-known insurance firm, and 2) a well-known gentlemen's club.

Yes, one of the applicants stripped for cash.

Gossip spread through my department as rapidly as the well-oiled thighs of an exotic dancer who spots a patron waving a $100 bill. Then word leaked out to other areas in my large company, creating a high-energy chain reaction of speculation, armchair quarterbacking and high-stakes office pools. Would Tobalski hire the mature, qualified, safe mother of three? Or the tart?

That often-used cliché, "Life's not always fair," applied to this particular applicant. First, she might not even be a dancer. Maybe she's the club's bookkeeper. Or the club's community-service coordinator who organizes car washes and candle sales for children's charities. She might even work undercover for the IRS and its small business tax-evasion unit. I shared all of these viable hypotheses with coworkers, and they tested poorly. Very poorly.

During the next several days, I obsessed over my quandary. Under what set of circumstances could I imagine myself actually hiring this young woman? Did I have the guts? Could I survive the avalanche of innuendoes and jokes from my male colleagues? How would I explain this hiring decision to my wife who, under normal circumstances, completely trusted me?

I eventually started rehearsing excuses that would explain to the young lady why she did not qualify for an in-person interview. They all sounded shallow and dishonest as I practiced them in my thoughts. This moral and ethical dilemma began to erode my physical and emotional health. The deterioration advanced slowly. I replaced my morning glass of freshly squeezed orange juice with seven pots of very black coffee. I substituted whistling and smiling with diarrhea and vomiting. Sometimes I wore the exact clothes from the day before . . . and the day before that. According to the office staff, my phone rang 15 to 20 times before I even noticed. My final, indignant moment occurred after I spilled some toner on the white tile floor while trying to service our copy machine and saw a vision of Isaac Hayes in the fine, granular mess. I needed help, lots of it, from people with six to 10 capital letters after their names.

Days passed while I wandered the long halls and back alleys, searching for direction, for answers, for some guiding light. I eventually visited myself in a dream one night where

I found the truth, hiding in its usual place—inside my soul. I was my own best mentor. The person I trusted was *me.*

After a stern lecture to myself, standing in front of the bathroom mirror with toothpaste foaming on my lips, I reached the following conclusion: she deserved a chance, an honest-to-goodness fighting opportunity to win this job.

We arranged to interview both candidates on the same day. A team of my staff would conduct a group interrogation, followed by a solo interview by me.

The big day arrived. Earlier that morning, I shaved with a straight razor, splashed on some cologne, trimmed a few nose hairs, ironed my boxer shorts and selected my smartest sport coat and tie. Just part of my traditional pre-interview routine.

First, we met with the older candidate. Salt of the earth. Lived on a countryside farm. Proud of her family. Loved hard work and an honest day's pay. Perfect fit for a group of younger employees who needed a second mom in their lives. All I would have to do is extend her a job offer then coast to retirement. As easy as a blink.

Next up . . . the younger woman. The prelude and anticipation were hypnotic. Minutes before she stepped into my office, I imagined her sitting across from me. Tall and lanky. Athletically narrowed face, set with tiger-eyes and slender lips. Olive tanned skin contrasted with a white blouse, buttons straining to stay in place, fighting the tension created by her firm attributes. Flowing, natural blond hair pulled back into a ponytail, tamed by a delicate scrunchy made of silver lace. Long, clear polished fingernails with white-accented tips. Nylon-less legs, crossed, her smooth right knee glistening under the overhead fluorescent lights. The room smelled like lemonade, cool and fresh. My throat became parched. I swallowed hard. But it didn't help.

I recovered from my mirage and pressed the intercom. It was time.

The exact second she walked through the doorway, my prophecy came alive. Every detail precise. Each memory clear. Except for one. I smelled a smooth Cabernet Sauvignon.

She was attractive, in a Hollywood-centerfold sort of way. Her beautiful eyes massaged whatever she looked at. Flowing blond hair rested on her perfect shoulders. All 6 feet of her moved in harmony. And the buttons on her blouse were stressed beyond the maximum allowed by the clothing manufacturer. It was impossible not to notice this, for any interviewer, male or female. It's what business people do with this information that varies.

First, I talked. Then, I listened. Then I talked again. This went on for about 60 minutes, with intermittent and rude interruptions from the extremely sarcastic voice inside my head. *Hire her! Nobody will talk behind your back. Work late! Your family trusts you. Her legs aren't that long! She types fast. It's her American right to own cleavage. Go ahead . . . stick a $20 bill under her belt. She knows shorthand! I'll support your decision.*

Sometimes my inner self acted like a major-league prick.

The interview ended after I explained health insurance benefits and vacation accrual. We shook hands and exchanged a few final pleasantries.

After she left, I ceremoniously created an Excel document with the headings of "pros" and "cons," which serves as an excellent decision-making tool for people-management nerds. I tried typing, but nothing traveled from my brain to my fingertips. I stared at my computer, my lifeless fingers on the keyboard. Finally, the screen saver turned on. I jiggled my mouse and stared again at the blank document. I played with my tape dispenser for a few minutes, fondled my stapler and tinkered with my three-hole punch. No, none of those objects is Freudian metaphor.

By now, word of my upcoming hiring dilemma had spread to every water cooler and break room in the corporation. Secret office pools and side wagers had sprung up everywhere. My pending decision brought more money into our company than total sales from the previous quarter. The accounting department's odds were 3 to 1 on the dancer.

Six days, five migraines, 10 chewed fingernails and one peptic ulcer later, I decided to hire the matronly applicant. After all, she was the best candidate, the person who would take my employees and me under her wing and nourish us with pleasant greetings and freshly baked cupcakes adorned with sweet sprinkles. And she turned out to be the right choice, for decades to come.

On the other hand, the guys from the loading docks hated me, taunted me, questioned the size of my manhood and hated me some more. But eventually they stopped urinating in the radiator of my car, once the head of engineering hired his own new assistant, who looked like Catherine Zeta-Jones from the chin up, Dolly Parton from neck to waistline and an ostrich from upper thighs to feet.

My decision was just that . . . my decision. I lived with the consequences, which were few, such as the occasional taxi ride when my car stalled once the urine reached the fuel line. At least I could hold my head high, in the privacy of my lonely office.

I occasionally think about the dance-club candidate, strictly from a humanitarian point of view. Did she break free from the shackles of sleaze? Maybe she earned enough tip money to attend college, complete a special-education degree and teach handicapped children their ABCs and 123s.

On the other hand, she might be turning tricks in the back of a rented U-Haul on weekends, under the dim light emanating from a cracked disco strobe light, to help feed her three kids and invalid grandmother. Could I live with that consequence? Then I remembered the fresh peach cobbler our secretary brought to work every first Monday of the month, kept warm by the knitted cozy she had made. The sweet manna melted in your mouth.

Jim recently retired from management, and staff honored him and his Wisconsin heritage with his own bobble-head doll.

The Unconventional Recruit

by
Julie Royce

Dressed in combat gear with a dummy rifle slung over my shoulder, I climbed the steps to the high diving board. The male FBI recruits who crowded around to watch me jump warned each other that when their turns came they should, "Hold tight to the family jewels," and "Go in straight—feet first. It will hurt less that way." They offered me no advice.

That's when my mind froze on one fact: I swam like a ton of reinforced concrete.

I searched the staring faces for glimmers of compassion—a slight smile, a worried look—some hint that I had an ally who wouldn't let me drown. The job posting hadn't mentioned swimming.

"You don't have to swim. You just have to flail to the side and haul your ass out," the instructor said.

I wanted to ask how many times an FBI agent had

jumped from a high-diving board in the line of duty, but it was too late for that. If I was going to die, I planned to do so with dignity. No tears, no groveling, no hesitation.

I walked to the end of the board and stepped over, staying as close to the side of the pool as possible. I sank in a split-second then rose at a speed that defied the theory of a body's natural buoyancy. I broke the surface, thrashing and spitting and sputtering—but close enough for a handhold. I took several deep, painful breaths before hoisting myself up and over the edge. I lay like a beached mermaid, grateful for the chlorine-permeated oxygen filling my lungs.

During those moments when death had seemed imminent, what flashed before my eyes wasn't my life, but how I got myself into that predicament. While my law school classmates applied to firms with fancy pedigrees, I sent my application to the Federal Bureau of Investigation. I thought the 14-week training program on the Marine Corps Base at Quantico sounded intriguing. I read subtext into the posting: Three meals a day with someone else assigned cleanup and a top-notch physical fitness program that I needed after years of studying late into the nights, with only bags of chips and tubs of onion dip to keep me company. Women paid big bucks to get into shape, but for me, the program would be free.

My dream of a little excitement seemed normal compared to the FBI rationale for hiring me. I stood 5 feet tall, weighed 110 pounds and had never done anything physical in my life. But I passed the background check, which confirmed that my neighbors said nice things about me and were unaware of any peculiar sexual proclivities. Our country's premier investigative agency confirmed I had no criminal record—I'd never even had a speeding ticket—and I didn't associate with known felons. I was hired.

I sold my condo in California, packed a couple of suits, a pair of running shoes and all of my 1960s' idealism into a suitcase and headed to an enclave a few miles outside of Washington, D.C. I was as naïve and green as Jed Clampett heading from Bug Tussle to Beverly Hills. My goal was to survive the on-the-job-training and get my credentials, a gun and a sexy new body.

My class had 10 women and 25 men, the largest proportion of women to men ever accepted into a new recruit class. It was the late 1970s, and the Bureau was under pressure to hire women and minorities. Up until then, diversity meant they hired white men from all 50 states. FBI old timers didn't welcome change. True Hooverites still genuflected during their morning two-mile runs on Hoover Road.

The men—new hires and agents alike—were politically conservative ex-cops, ex-marines, ex-special-forces and other ex-military. Conservative women stayed clear of the FBI unless they married an agent. We were 10 females, big on constitutional rights, big on limiting search and seizure, big on strengthening the requirements for probable cause . . . idealism that the FBI didn't appreciate.

A newly-minted lawyer, I was also big on logic. Events and actions had to make sense. I soon learned that conduct logical to me didn't always appear that way to my instructors. Their lack of common sense proved painful.

My male classmates had been trained by the best. Under other circumstances, they might have been considered an exceptional dating pool: bright, buffed, physically fit and full of testosterone. I struggled with 10 pushups, climbing a 12-foot rope to scale a wall or a single unmodified pull-up.

Our instructors—think Lou Gossett Jr. as the marine drill sergeant in *An Officer and a Gentleman*—devised a ready list of tortures. I figured I could put up with any persecution for three and a half months.

The first day in the gym, we double-timed around the perimeter until I gasped for air. Then the fun began. As we slumped to the floor, the women in varying stages of exhaustion, the instructor began. "Snake Henderson stands 6-feet 6-inches, has a jagged 5-inch scar down his left cheek, eats small babies for breakfast and has killed at least a hundred tough guys. He takes no prisoners. He makes Bad, Bad Leroy Brown look like a wimp. You'll meet him on a dark street corner, and you'd better be able to take care of yourself because he wants you dead. Keeping you alive is what defensive tactics are about."

I was impressed.

To ready me for a confrontation with Mr. Henderson, we engaged in boxing. Boxing, for God's sake. Do you think Snake Henderson is going to box with me? Do you think he's going to give me a helmet and gloves? Determined to be a team player, I kept the logic glitch to myself.

I was paired with Pete. He delivered a right uppercut, and my head bounced off the sides of that damned helmet like a steel ball shot in a pinball machine. It was an hour before

I could think clearly. My roommate said I kept mumbling something that sounded like, "Team player. Team player."

A week later, we tried a new exercise. "Pair off. One of you runs one way, one of you the other, circle the gym and when you meet, grab your opponent and flip him over your shoulder."

"Wait, I'm paired up with Jack. He's a foot taller and has 100 pounds on me. The fundamentals of leverage say this isn't going to work."

"Quit whining. Do you think Snake Henderson will cut you any slack?"

"No, but I don't think I'm going to argue with Snake if he comes at me ready for the kill. Isn't that why you give me a gun?"

His frown said, "Run!"

OK, OK. I'm a team player. What's the worst thing that could happen? I thought. I loped forward. *Let Jack get worn out running.* When we finally met, I heard a choir of onlookers screaming, "Bite him! Bite him!" And I did.

That made sense—was imminently logical. Biting, scratching and clawing eyes are fair play in a street fight with the formidable Snake Henderson, who had no respect for proper rules of gentlemanly conduct. But Jack didn't see it that way. The onlookers frowned as though I'd committed an unpardonable sin. Apparently they were yelling, "Fight him! Fight him!" Not, "Bite him! Bite him!"

Two weeks later, Jack evened the score, although I'm sure it was unintentional. He flipped me. His head came up as my nose went down. There was a very loud *crack*! Jack apologized to me. Then he apologized to the instructor who was too busy cleaning my blood off the floor to pay him much attention. Later that night, with my nose and eyes swollen, I convinced Jack it was more than OK, it was the best thing that had happened to me since I'd been at Quantico; the doctor gave me an excuse to sit out of boxing for the next four weeks.

I enjoyed firearms training. Mostly. I do wish someone had told me to hold the shotgun tight to my shoulder. It would have reduced the bruising. But firearms would prove to be my downfall. I had no problem with the rifles, the shotguns, the two-handed .38 course. But the heft of the gun and the recoil on the one-handed revolver course was too much to let my small, weak hand bring the gun back into alignment to shoot again. "I'm fine when I use two hands," I said.

"And what will you do when Snake Henderson shoots you in your left hand, and you have to protect yourself?"

There it was. The last logic glitch I'd have to swallow before leaving Quantico. "You assume he shoots me in the non-dominant hand, not the head or some other vital body part?" I asked. "You assume I'm bleeding profusely from that non-dominant hand? You assume I'm already down and panicked? Yet you believe shooting one-handed is going to save me?"

"Just shoot," he said.

"Local law enforcement agencies don't make trainees pass a one-handed course."

"This is the FBI. Shoot," he said again.

"Hey, look, I could prop it against my left forearm, bloody though it is from my wound. I'm sure adrenaline would kick in."

I was unable to pass the one-handed firearms course, and the FBI politely asked me to leave. I was 5 pounds lighter, could flex real muscle and I'd learned a few new tricks. So what if I couldn't shoot one-handed? I couldn't imagine another job where my boss would care.

FBI training at Quantico, circa 1970s

What *Not* to Wear to Work

by
Kim Parsells

I was 19 years old, fresh out of art school and cocky as hell when I landed my first real job. I had just received my two-year degree in music/video business from the Art Institute of Seattle and had temporarily moved back to a small town in Idaho to save a little money before heading off to Nashville to hit it big.

Wanting to utilize my—what I now know in hindsight to be utterly ridiculous—education, I applied for a job as a radio sales representative. Radio people are different, and this was an absolute stroke of luck for me. In radio, there is a combination of passion for both music and business that exists in few other industries.

When asked during the initial interview what I would spend my first paycheck on, I answered, "A guitar." In almost any other type of business, this would have been grounds for

"Thank you. We'll be in touch . . . never." It got me hired in radio.

After four weeks, I was well-enough trained in sales to be unleashed onto the community. I was meeting my quota and everything was going along pretty smoothly. I had made a few friends at the station and did not find it odd when one of the other sales ladies asked to borrow my go-go boots for a costume party. She was older by 10 years, so I excused her for not owning a pair, much less thinking they were for a costume.

The station manager—who was also the wife of the station owner—had an enormous appreciation for name-brand labels, expensive jewelry and fine wine. So, when she greeted me daily with a long, slow, hair-to-shoe glance, I could only assume that she was admiring my unique sense of style on a budget.

I had the good sense to buy only black clothes, so there were no real faux pas when it came to mixing and matching. My makeup was one or two shades lighter than my natural skin tone. I loved the way it made the thick black liner around my eyes pop. My mom told people I was going through a "goth" phase, but I believed this look to be both elegant and classy.

On a Tuesday afternoon, after five weeks of employment, I was called into the station manager's office. She made no small talk and got straight to the point. She simply looked at me and said, "Go home and change. If I see you wearing all black again, I will fire you."

I was too stunned to be humiliated. I explained I could

go home and change, but all I owned were black clothes. She gave me $100 in cash and instructed me to go to Macy's and to ask the saleslady what would be appropriate to wear to work. As I walked out the door, she added, "It wouldn't hurt to stop by the makeup counter, too."

To this day, I utilize many of the sales techniques I learned during my two-year stint there. I have never used my college degree, and I own only one black sweater.

Goth-phase photos unavailable.

Kim's mother destroyed them.

Man of Steel

by
Don Stewart

I'm pretty sure I failed the test that day, unless survival is enough to get you a passing grade. Even so, the experience of watching solid rock cook into liquid steel became a turning point in my life, a memorable milestone. My personal trial by fire, you could say, with a toxic dose of nicotine for flavor.

My father believed that anyone privileged enough to expect a life on the affluent side of the railroad tracks ought to spend some time earning a real wage in a blue-collar job. Backing up philosophy with action, he arranged for me to spend the summer of my sophomore year in college working in a steel yard.

As an apprentice industrial insulator, my job was to haul tools and material around the construction site of the world's newest, most technologically advanced blast furnace, wrapping layers of rock wool and fiberglass onto miles of steam and water pipes that ran throughout the complex. My other job, the one not written on the application, was to learn how to be a man.

Nine stories tall, the Number Eight Blast Furnace stood at the end of a mile-long queue of mammoth structures that rose belching from the ground like gigantic bishops on a colossal chessboard. Number Eight was so powerful, they said, that the waste heat of its exhaust would be channeled away in 10-foot-wide conduits to three adjacent furnaces, there to be inhaled as auxiliary fuel.

Railroad tracks ran the length of the facility, with spurs and sidelines serving the long row of furnaces. Cars carried in tons of raw ore, coal and limestone and retreated with cauldrons full of molten steel. Close by, giant front-end loaders and heavy diesel dump trucks worked in endless shifts, scooping and hauling mountains of slag, lumps of burnt limestone and ore. The entire complex was busy, noisy and perilous. And it was hot.

That year had ushered in a dry summer. Weeks without rain brought on the worst drought the South had experienced in any man's lifetime. The temperature taunted the 110-degree mark for a week, and finally surpassed that toasty line one late-July afternoon.

My task that day was to affix pre-formed fiberglass tubes onto a long stretch of steam pipe, one of three pipes that ran from the fourth-story superstructure of the new furnace to a building all the way across the rail yard and disappeared flush into the building's bare, sheet metal wall.

Our butts slid along on the lowest of the three pipes,

safety harnesses clipped to the pipe behind our heads. The day's work involved nothing more than removing pre-fab sections of split fiberglass tubing from a box, slipping them onto the pipe suspended at eye-level in front of us, and sealing the joints with aluminized duct tape. We pushed the large cardboard boxes ahead of us as we scooted along in the heat, clamping and taping, yard-by-yard.

Fiberglass—the active ingredient in novelty itching powder—can be irritating to work with, even under the best of conditions. Hot weather does nothing to lessen the effect of microscopic bits of spun glass that stick to your sweat and work their way into your skin, creep into eyelids and nostrils or fly straightaway into your lungs. The stuff is miserable.

We took precautions, of course—long sleeves and gloves were essential, with shirts buttoned all the way up and bandanas tied firmly in place to keep the dust off our necks. Hard hats were required on the work site, and safety glasses, too. Facemasks—the surgical kind, with the rubber-band straps—were highly encouraged.

Bundled head to toe in protective clothing on the hottest day of the year, we were suspended 50 feet above an expanse of busy railroad track, where we were periodically roasted by the passage of 8-foot-wide cauldrons of sloshing red pig iron.

It was under this precarious set of conditions that the journeyman looked at me and asked, "You ever dip Skoal, boy?"

"Never." Oh, I had tasted cigarettes before. Cigars, too. My eighth-grade buddy and I had once scored a couple of fat El Productos and spent one lazy summer afternoon in his room puffing on them in a sincere effort to demonstrate to each other that we actually knew what we were doing. We rolled them between our fingers knowingly, struggling to blow smoke rings while discussing worldly issues, like what girls really wanted us to do with them, if we ever got the chance. This experiment fast became no fun at all, though, as our mouths began to burn and our stomachs turned queasy, something neither of us was willing to admit to the other.

"I think I'll save some of this for later," I said, tapping out my stogie in the plastic Tonka wheel we were using for an ashtray. "Gotta go home anyway."

And just in time, too. As I headed out the back door to grab my bike, my friend's mother came in the front, hours earlier than expected. On reflex, he tossed his lit cigar under his bed, where it set fire to a pile of dust bunnies, adding to the already-hazy atmosphere of his room.

Her punishment was cruel, but effective. She made him retrieve the smoldering cigar from under the bed and smoke it completely, inhaling every puff, while she watched. Then she gently held his forehead while he emptied his guts into the toilet bowl. Tough love, for sure.

To my knowledge, he never smoked again. The experience turned me away from cigars as well, and thanks to my father's four-pack-a-day habit, I never developed a fondness for cigarettes, either. Before that day at the steel mill, though, I had never, ever dipped snuff.

That hot July afternoon, I turned to find my boss— Tommy was his name, or maybe Jimmy or Billy— offering a thin round tin full of chopped black tobacco, opened for my inspection and sampling. With it, he provided detailed verbal instructions describing the proper technique for placing a big pinch between lower lip and gum. "Don't get any on your tongue," he said. "Don't swallow the spit. Spit the spit. Hell. No, don't spit out the snuff, just the spit. Might get a bit spicy, but don't fret—it'll go away in a minute when your cheek gets numb . . . "

I forget the rest. It only took seconds for saliva to well up until it spilled out of my eyes, for concentrated tobacco juice to seep between my teeth and coat my tongue with pure, bitter fire. A split second later, my head inflated like a cheap helium balloon, and it began to spin of its own accord about my shoulders. I wanted to cry. I wanted to throw up. But most of all, I wanted to spit that crap out of my mouth as fast as I had shoved it in. Faster even. But Jim-Bill-Bud-Tommy had other ideas. His opinion held sway, given the manly code of conduct that ruled the worksite, his seniority as journeyman to my apprentice and the fact that he barred the only exit route from my tenuous perch high above the smoking railroad tracks.

I looked to my right, where the pipes disappeared into the building across the yard. No escape there. The wall seemed to waver in the afternoon sun, bending and swaying in the stifling heat that rose from below. Time slowed, the way it does when you are about to leave the highway, roll your car, crash into oncoming traffic. My stomach turned over, didn't much care for its new position and turned again, once more in the wrong direction. My arms and legs went limp. My head simply decided to stop spinning and swim away. I was already sweating.

A stiff gust of arid wind suddenly lifted an empty box a foot or so into the air, tipped it over and let it go, slow motion, a huge corrugated feather tumbling down into the glowing, orange maw of the slopping-full cauldron passing directly below us. I watched in utter fascination, my face aglow from the sun above, the molten iron below and rising levels of nicotine deep within, as the big box touched down onto a rippling surface of liquid metal.

Whooof! In the space of a second, it was gone.

It didn't just burn. It disappeared. That box simply was not any more. It had vanished in a single puff, in a surreal, 6-foot curl of orange flame, without a trace of ash. The vision was both fascinating and horrifying—especially when I realized that I was next. Without my say-so, my body gradually began easing forward in the heat, slumping down toward the magnetic pull of the red-hot train car. My face relaxed, my mouth fell open and the bulk of the tobacco spilled from my lips.

Soon, hands were upon me, initiating a cloudy series of events and a buzz of conversation that somehow culminated in my safe return to the ground. I vaguely recall a flurry of coarse utterances, some inquiring as to my welfare, but most involving the words "pussy" and "college boy" before a Dixie cone of ice water splashed in my face and brought me back around.

"Go home, tough guy," said the foreman, without a hint of sympathy in his voice, once he was sure I could walk well enough to make it to my car, "and be back here tomorrow. Early."

What Comes First?

by

Patricia Mayes

When I retired from a longtime career in nursing, mostly in Hospice care, I didn't envision raising chickens and selling eggs. This second career was an accident of sorts: the chickens came first, and then the eggs. But one evening, I paid the price of dignity for those eggs and my new occupation.

In the spring, I moved into a house that had a very nice chicken coop out back, but no chickens. All summer long, in between unpacking boxes and thinking about how to squeeze stuff from a five-bedroom house into a house with three tiny bedrooms, I sat on my back patio and gazed at the chicken coop. I visualized a yard full of clucking chickens and thought about the wonderful fertilizer I could have for my gardens. So I sold my extra stuff and bought chickens with the proceeds.

It's important for you to know I was new to the skill

of raising chickens and selling eggs, and it was a skill I was not taught in nursing school. In the fall, I set about learning everything I could about raising chickens for eggs, and I started getting the hen-house bedroom ready for my 16 new boarders: Grace, Betty, Alice, Agnes, Gertrude, Helen, Olivia, Ruth, Joan, Francis, Joyce, Ollie, Macie, Sarah, Elizabeth and Marie.

I'm usually very careful, or damn lucky. In my need for independence, I carry my own version of the "I've-fallen-and-can't-get-up" safety net—a cellphone. Never walking out the door without it in a pocket was a ritual, except for a quick trip to the henhouse one night to gather the last of the eggs and give the girls a little bedtime snack.

It was bitterly cold that night, so I slipped on a sweater over my nightgown. My sweater had no pockets, and no pockets meant no way to carry my cellphone. Planning to be gone only a few minutes, I saw no need for it, so I headed out.

Once finished with my chicken chores inside the henhouse, I placed the bag of meal worms back onto the shelf and attempted to open the door. The knob wouldn't turn! It was locked. I had no key and no phone. I was locked in the henhouse in nothing but my nightgown, a sweater and my chicken-shit-wading boots.

The horror set in slowly. In my zeal to keep raccoons and foxes out of the henhouse where they could kidnap one of my girls and not demand a ransom, I reversed the deadbolt lock on the door and used it for nighttime use only. It could only be opened from the outside, with a key. Somehow, the lock tripped itself when I closed the door.

Now this new chicken owner had become a dumb cluck. There I was, locked in the henhouse on a cold winter night with a basket of eggs and 16 chickens that I would never kill to stay alive, no phone and no immediately-obvious way to get out. I shivered in my flannel nightgown.

Giving up was not an option. While I cussed at myself for being so stupid, I looked around for a tool to whack my way out. My first option was the chicken-poop scraper. Not having any luck using the blade to pry open the lock, my next choice was the brick on which the Flock-Block treat was sitting. I decided that since I had broken the blade of the poop-scraper, the mortar brick would do the trick to break a hinge on the door. Not so. The brick shattered into pieces with the first whack. My third and last choice was to use one of the nails holding up the barn heater to pry the pin out of the door hinge. Each nail bent on the first try.

Then I calmly considered the very real possibility that I—who depended on these chickens and their eggs for my new career—might die in the henhouse with them. I wondered how long it would take for anyone to miss me; with no schedule to keep, no official job to show up to every day, and my many road trips on which I took off without letting anyone know, it could be a week or more before I would be missed.

I surveyed my surroundings, and the chickens surveyed me. They appeared happy to have their momma joining them for an impromptu slumber party. Telling them everything would be OK, I calmed myself, knowing I'd be OK on water for a while since I had just filled the five-gallon water can. And I reasoned I could eat raw eggs, as long as the girls continued to put out. The temperature in the henhouse was a comfortable 64 degrees, and there was clean straw to sleep on. The chickens peed and pooped in the henhouse, so I felt comfortable claiming a far corner for my personal use . . . a "my-space, your-space" kind of thing.

As my predicament settled into my disbelieving mind, I sat down on the huge hunk of Flock Block and bawled my eyeballs out. I was going to die in a henhouse in my flannel nightie, wearing boots covered in chicken shit. Printed on my tombstone would be, "Here lies Pat, she clucked with the best," with a picture of a chicken engraved in the granite.

After I finished my crying jag, I blew my nose on one end of my fancy flannel nightie and wiped my tears on the sleeve of my sweater. In doing so, I looked up and realized my imaginary death trap had a window—albeit a small one—8 feet off the floor. *Can I get out of here after all?* I asked myself. Hope and joy and a burst of energy filled every fiber of my being. *But how am I going to get up to the window?!*

The window looked tiny from where I sat, and I didn't know if I would be able to reach it. Then survival instinct—which incites people to lift cars, leap over roofs and go through flames—kicked in. I ripped the chicken-roost ladder from its railing, only to realize it was designed for a 6-pound chicken, not a 180-pound person. Plan A, gone.

Then I had another idea, thanks to the old farmer at the feed store who had sent me to Goodwill to buy used cat carriers for nesting boxes. He said, "They're portable, sturdy and easy to clean." What he didn't say was that they could be used as a ladder of sorts. I figured that if I stacked three of them just so, I could maybe reach that window enough to hoist myself up and through it, even if I had to take the remnants of the poop scraper and bricks to bust it open. Nothing could stop me now.

After many attempts at stacking cat carriers and falling back onto the floor of the henhouse, I was successful on my fifth try. I had reached the window and freedom was near! That's when realization hit—my hips were wider than the window.

The last time I had the courage to measure my hips was on my 68th birthday. They came in at 47 and 1/4 inches! What was downright depressing about those inches—nearly 4 feet of them—was that I was only 5 feet 2 inches tall. My hips were almost as wide as I was tall and represented a new definition of "middle-age spread."

The law of physics and my nursing background took over—all I needed was a lubricant and some common sense. *Everything has to slide somewhere*, I thought, and I was covered with chicken shit. Plus, I had delivered hundreds of babies in my nursing career. They usually came out head first with a lot of turning, twisting and sliding in fluids. All I needed to do was put my head and shoulders through the narrow window and then, ever-so-gently but firmly, massage my massive hips through the opening . . . just like birthing a baby. Easy! After all, I had done this four times while giving birth to my children. I could do it once more.

Reaching through the window, I grabbed the eave of

the potting shed that was next to the coop. *Breathe. Push. Breathe Push. Just like childbirth.*

Cat carriers flew. Chickens flew. My head, shoulders and waist were through the window, and I was perched on the inside of the potting shed, trapped by my hips. Oh, those hips! It took quite a while to twist, turn, push, first one hip, then the other, all the while saying under my breath, "It's just like giving birth or laying an egg, depending on whether one is a human or a chicken. You can do this. PUSH HARD!"

After one last deep breath and push, I was free. I landed on the potting-shed floor amid a pile of garden hoses and broken flowerpots. The door to the potting shed was open, and I could feel the chill of the night's winter air rush over my putrid-smelling, hot body. What a blessed feeling. I convulsed with laughter—that is, until I peed all over myself in happiness.

After I caught my breath, I uncoiled the garden hoses from my legs, arms and neck and tried to shake straw and shards of pottery from my hair and gown. I gave up on doing anything about the chicken shit. That would take a lot of soap and scrubbing.

Somewhere in the melee, I had lost the boots, so I was happily barefooted as I plodded out of the shed, unlocked the door to the chicken coop, picked up my eggs and boots and told the girls goodnight.

Once inside my house, I scribbled a note and taped it to the inside of the back door: "Where is your phone?" Next, I deposited my clothes in the washing machine then took a long shower. My hair still smells like the chicken coop when the wind blows just right.

When I had cleaned up, I got the eggs ready for the next day's customers. I gently washed each one and placed them onto a rack to air-dry overnight. As I worked, I smiled to myself over the thought that none of my customers would appreciate—or believe—what I had gone through in my new business venture.

Patricia's granddaughter Sarah with Mazie and the other chickens. Sarah is wearing Grandma's chicken-mucking boots, the same ones from the story.

Slam Dunk

by
Juli Alexieff

My day started as normal as any other when the alarm went off. I staggered into the shower then made myself look presentable at zero-dark-thirty. I kissed the dog and hubby goodbye—in that order—and drove by remote to my new job in the fast-paced, high-stress pre-surgical care unit.

Once dressed in my Smurf-blue scrubs, I loaded up my laptop, brought up the day's surgery schedule and turned up the volume on my link to society—my hospital-provided cellphone. My phone went with me wherever I roamed so that I was always just a call away from the beckoning wails of surgeons in distress over their use of computerized order-entry.

Once settled in for the long haul of my 12-hour shift, I began my routine of order placement, paper pushing and email sending. While becoming absorbed by the day-to-day duties, I considered the hours ahead and prayed that nothing out of the norm would fall from the sky and onto my head on this, the final day of three very long shifts. My go-to gal—who was also my stretched-to-the-max manager—was away at a leadership conference, my IT guru was out ill and lord knows the unit secretary couldn't dare to spare a second of her precious time if I indeed found myself in a quandary and needed assistance. So basically, I was on my own.

Except I was not really alone. I had my cellphone—the same phone that made me jump whenever it rang, the same phone that made me break out into a sweat whenever I saw a doctor's name come across the display screen.

My new job had many perks, but the cellphone was NOT one of them, for with it came trouble—trouble that I was supposed to deflect, eradicate, repair and defeat. As physician concierge/scribe for the surgical services team, it was my responsibility to problem-solve; however, I was still learning how to douse fires and usually it was something a tired, grizzled, frayed surgeon did not want or need to hear. I was his link to the land of computerized order-entry, and when the phone rang, I knew I'd better answer it.

It was getting late in the afternoon, and the clock told me the day was winding down. I was happy I could make it through another day without being unveiled as the physician-concierge fraud I sometimes thought myself to be. Though I knew I did good work and represented myself with professionalism and knowledge, I was still so unsure of myself.

On that day, my last of three, I got a call from dear old Mother Nature. I grabbed my phone, placed it in the top pocket of my scrubs and made my way to the ladies' locker room. When finished, I hastily turned, leaned over and hit the flusher. At that moment, time stood still as I watched in wonder—my lifeline to those surgeons made a slam dunk into the swirling waters below, disappearing from sight. Instead of dousing fires, I had drowned my phone.

In a valiant effort, I threw caution to the wind and plunged my arm down into the frigid waters, reaching into the bowels of the drain. Unfortunately, I was too late. My phone had been sucked out to sea. That's when I realized the norm had just fallen from the sky and smacked me upside the head.

I made a mad dash back to my workstation, all the while believing I would surely plug the whole hospital sewer system and be responsible for the million-dollar repairs. I immediately placed a frantic call to the engineering department and tried to remain calm while I explained the situation. I was rewarded with a, "Well, way to go. Now you've done it," followed by a big laugh. Seems I wasn't the first to flush a phone down the drain, nor probably the last.

My next call was to the IT guys since I needed a replacement phone. They informed me that a request would have to be sent to my manager, who was, unfortunately, at her leadership conference. They told me that a loaner phone would be delivered in the interim, but that the $500 cost of the phone would have to be authorized before a new one could be sent over. It was at that moment that I wished for my lifeline—I really needed to call a friend.

Instead, I sent an email to my hopefully not-soon-to-be

ex-manager, explained the mishap and told her why she had received a purchasing request for a $500 replacement phone. I packed my personal belongings, changed out of my Smurf-blue scrubs and drove home. Once there, I reached out to the one person who would understand not only my concern and embarrassment over the situation, but also the humor of it—my mom! I called her and she listened to my fears of reprimand or worse. We shared a laugh over the freakish chance of losing my phone in the toilet. With this one call to my true lifeline, all my worries disappeared. Thank goodness, I had one link to society that had not gone down the drain.

I lived to work another day as the surgical services physician concierge/scribe, and from that day forward, I left the beckoning wails of the surgeons on my desk whenever nature called.

A slam dunk

A Martini Mishap

by
Frank Masi

I thought the day would never come. After selling computer products for three years in Manhattan, I was ready for a promotion, and my company was opening a new branch office in White Plains, New York. I made my usual morning call from my territory to the office to retrieve messages, and the office secretary, Lisa DiLissi, said, "The boss wants to talk to you. Come on in after lunch." It was raining, and I had a bad cold, but when the boss calls, you don't say no.

My sales had been so good that as I drove to the office, I immediately surmised the boss was going to give me the bad news that deliveries would be late. This would slow down my commission payout.

"Congratulations," he said, as I sat in front of him, ready for trouble. "We're promoting you to sales manager for our new White Plains office."

I sneezed as he said it and thought that maybe I hadn't heard him right. So I blurted out through a stuffed nose and scratchy throat, "Me? I'm the new sales manager?"

"Yes, Frank. You've done a heck of a sales job, and we need someone who can hit the ground running to make an early success of our new office. Who better than our star salesman?"

I left his office in a daze, giddy from the promotion and head spinning from my cold. That's when Lisa announced to me that she and the other seven sales reps, all men, were going to help me celebrate by taking me out for martinis—my favorite cocktail—at a swanky singles bar right around the corner from our Manhattan office. In spite of my head-clogged, nose-running condition, I agreed. I couldn't refuse, especially since they mixed the best dry martinis in the city—with three olives, to boot!

I couldn't hold down food all day, but the office team managed to pump six martinis into me by 8 P.M. and that did the trick. My brain was drowning in Beefeater gin, and I could barely stand upright.

My girlfriend, Cora, who also worked at the company, was working late that night and couldn't join us for the celebration. So the guys virtually carried me home to my small, one-bedroom apartment just six blocks from our office, with Lisa tagging along.

Once in my apartment, the boys undressed me, but it was Lisa who played the motherly role and tucked me in. At that moment, the telephone in my apartment rang. It was my girlfriend, Cora. For some reason apparent only to the Party Gods, it was Lisa who picked up the phone. Cora knew Lisa from the company and recognized her voice immediately, prompting my girlfriend to ask, "Lisa, what are you doing in Frank's apartment?"

Lisa responded, "I was just getting Frank into bed."

It took a whole lot of explaining and creativity, even for a skilled salesman, to convince Cora later about the circumstances leading up to Lisa putting me to bed. I don't know if I ever succeeded.

When a KISS is Not a Kiss

by
Fred Hudgin

I was teaching my first data processing officer course at the Army Institute of Administration at Fort Harrison, Indiana. I'd been a second lieutenant for all of six months. My class of 29 officers ranged in rank from second lieutenant up to lieutenant colonel.

We were a few days into their introduction to the CO-BOL computer-programming language. Many of the young officers had already taken computer programming while they were in college. For this reason, those young men and women charged ahead with energy and easy success. The older officers struggled.

The army, in its wisdom, had decided that all of its officers, especially combat officers, had to have a second non-combat specialty. The data processing officer course was the plum that everyone tried to get into. The problem was that those senior officers were not good with details. They had grown used to making decisions then delegating the specifics to their staffs. As such, detail-oriented parts of their brains had gotten a little rusty from non-use.

Computer programming is a detail-oriented field. It was a little hard for those captains, majors and the lieutenant colonel to accept that the young lieutenants could excel at something while they, as older officers, could not. So they tried harder.

They were making all of the mistakes that new programmers make. Their solutions were far too complicated. They regularly boxed themselves into a blind alley with their programs. What they should have done was back up to correct their design then re-code from the corrected design. A bad design can never become a good program, and what they did was to add onto what they had already written, making it more and more difficult.

Finally, out of frustration, I tried to get their attention by using an acronym that I had learned in my officer basic class three months earlier. The army has acronyms for everything, and if you use an acronym, your credibility immediately soars by at least 50 percent. In fact, people have made careers in the army out of creating and using acronyms.

"Class," I announced to them proudly, "remember the KISS principle."

They all paused from their efforts and looked up at me. I could see in their eyes that they were ready for the new second lieutenant to say something stupid. Everyone knew that KISS meant, "Keep it simple, stupid."

As I began my explanation of the KISS principle, the

definition of the acronym was necessary. I said, "KISS means 'Keep it simple . . . '"

Then, I caught myself. I looked into the eyes of the lieutenant colonel and knew if I finished the phrase, I would be in deep shit. There was no way that a second lieutenant could get away with calling a collection of captains, majors and a lieutenant colonel, "Stupid."

The lieutenant colonel looked at me with amusement, clearly wondering how I was going to salvage my lesson. My pause grew longer and longer, and my face got redder and redder. The whole class was silent. Everyone in the room knew how the acronym ended and just as clearly that I had put myself into a spot.

Finally, a captain in the front row raised his hand. I called on him, and he answered, "Keep it simple, *sir*."

He saved my butt.

I used that acronym and definition in every class I taught after that, always drawing out the suspense of the last word before saying, "sir." It got a laugh every single time. After those officers graduated and began their military careers as Data Processing Officers, I hoped they remembered getting KISSed in COBOL class and kept their solutions simple.

Making the Grade

High marks for educators!

In Memory of Dazzle

by
Lola Di Giulio De Maci

"The fish is dead!"

Those were the first four words I heard one morning when I entered my second-grade classroom.

Oh, great, I thought. *A dead fish!* Right then I knew it was going to be a long day. I had 101 things on my to-do list. I didn't need a dead fish.

Sam, who loved researching anything on Attila the Hun, stood at attention with a net ready to scoop the departed fish out of the tank.

"Shall I flush him down the toilet?" he asked. "Or throw him in the trash can?"

I couldn't think fast enough. *What does one do with a fish that's left the pond?* Because death might be a new experience for some of the students—and since I didn't want the toilet-trash-can thing—I suggested we bury him. After all,

Dazzle deserved a proper burial for having been a classroom-friendly goldfish.

My mind raced. *What should Dazzle be placed in for burial? Where do we bury him? What do we dig the grave with? What kind of service should we hold? Will I get in trouble if I bring up the "God of Dead Fish" in a eulogy?*

The kids were upset, and I needed grown-up support and direction. So I decided to call the school office. I was careful how to phrase my questions because 20 grief-stricken second graders were at my side, listening to every word I said.

"We have a dead fish in our room," I heard myself say. "His name is Dazzle, and we want to bury him." I told the staff what had just happened and that I wanted to do right by the kids and Dazzle. I then asked about any procedures I should follow in meeting the school's rules. That is, if they had any for this kind of occasion.

Giggles turned to laughter on the other end of the line.

"Hey, you guys, this isn't funny," I whispered into the mouthpiece. "We're in mourning here."

After the giggling subsided in the office, we received instructions as to what we were permitted to do with the body. With that, the class and I headed outdoors to the soft dirt that would be Dazzle's final resting place.

Having picked a burial plot, we proceeded to place Dazzle in a napkin and dig the grave with a white plastic spoon. We then decided to honor him with a song.

"What shall we sing?" I asked 20 solemn apprentices. One of the kids started singing *God Bless America*.

"Oh, no!" I interrupted abruptly, and then realized I should have let him sing it through. But we were running out of time. "We don't need a flag song," I said apologetically. "We need a fish song."

The class didn't know a fish song. So Crystal—the classroom soloist and future Diana Ross—composed one on the spot. We all listened intently.

"The fish is d-e-e-e-a-d!" she sang, swaying to and fro, her face pointing heavenward. "The fish is d-e-e-e-a-d!"

I followed her song with the eulogy.

"I really didn't know you well, Dazzle," I began, "but I'm sure you were a good fish. Everyone in the class thought you were a good fish, too. We'll miss you."

Just then, I heard a little voice to my right say, "I know who killed you, Dazzle. It was Bubbles." Bubbles was Dazzle's roommate in the tank. It was hard to keep my composure—I didn't want to be like the gigglers at the other end of the phone earlier that morning.

When the service was over, it was time for recess. I welcomed a change of pace and a chance to look over the day's lesson plans. Wailing, ear-piercing sounds suddenly interrupted my thoughts.

"Dazzle is gone! Someone stole Dazzle!"

Someone had gone to the soft dirt where Dazzle lay and dug him up. The kids were traumatized and immediately went into mourning once again.

Now what? I thought.

We gathered in a group on the classroom rug, sitting in a circle, holding hands. We talked openly about our beloved pet and what he had meant to each of us. When all was said and done, the class decided that Bubbles was innocent and that he would be the new class mascot.

It was also decided that someone would have to feed Bubbles, clean his tank and take care of him. Sam volunteered for the job. But first . . . he would make sure there was enough time in his day to research Attila the Hun.

Lola in the classroom

Persuasion

by
Samantha Ducloux Waltz

"How many of you have given a persuasive speech?" I asked my communication skills class, forcing an upbeat tone of voice.

"Speech?" One of the boys straightened in his chair. "Like the president?"

"Persuasive?" someone else asked. "Like when I want to borrow my dad's car?"

Six weeks into the school year, this was the most interest I'd seen from my 12 high school juniors. My heart fluttered with hope. "You already know how to do it. You'll be great."

"I'm never great," James, the tallest and lankiest of the group, muttered.

My heart stilled. I bet all the students felt like James and I dreaded the task of trying to inspire them. This was the class no teacher wanted, including me, despite its small size.

These boys didn't qualify for special education, but had limited reading and writing skills attributed to a lack of motivation. I'd stayed awake nights trying to think of something that would capture their interest and had come up with this unit where each of them could study a topic of personal interest.

"You might surprise yourselves," I said. "A good persuasive speech gets your audience to agree with your thesis. Think about how you persuade a girl to go out with you or talk your mom into buying the shoes you want."

One boy yawned.

I inhaled. "Think of a thesis you feel strongly about. For example, 'Marijuana should be legalized for anyone to use.'"

Their eyes widened.

"You're in favor of that?" one student blurted.

"If I'm not, the facts you unearth and the way you deliver them can change my mind." I could imagine what they'd tell their parents about their English teacher. If they had parents at home. I knew students with histories of academic failure often came from chaotic households, and I felt a stab of sympathy for these boys.

"Another thesis might be, 'The school district should build a skateboard park for students,'" I said.

"Cool. They have soccer fields and baseball diamonds. They should give us a skate park, too."

"There's room down by the tennis courts," another boy added.

As the ideas grew, so did the sound. Good things could happen with these boys after all.

"Another topic might be lifting curfew laws."

"Everybody knows curfew is dumb," James said. "Some kids get picked on and some don't."

"So again, your homework is to come up with a thesis. You can choose any topic you want as long as you can support it and it's not X-rated. And come up with a backup idea in case someone beats you to your first choice."

Gone were the blank stares. I could see their minds churning.

I passed out assignment sheets and went over them. "You'll have to defend your idea with facts from three written sources. Books, magazines—be careful that something printed off the Internet is a reliable source. We'll go to the library as a class to do research."

Predictably, they groaned. Possibly none of these students had been in the library since freshman orientation.

"You'll have three to five minutes for your speech."

"Three to five minutes?" a student objected. "That's how long I need to eat lunch."

"Be sure to keep a bibliography of your sources."

"Bibliography? Isn't that a book about a person?"

"The format is on your assignment sheet."

I passed out evaluation forms they'd use to grade each other on their thesis statement, organization, research and delivery.

Their eyes glazed over at the word, "grade." Still, everyone came the next day with a thesis. The classroom buzzed with excitement. The boys quickly claimed ideas I'd thrown out the day before and came up with others. So much for labels of "troublemaker" and "failure."

When I asked James for his thesis, he spoke with a tone almost defiant. "Students should be allowed to chew in school."

A hush fell over the room.

I suspected many of the boys kept a wad of Copenhagen tucked inside their cheeks. Could I encourage their habit and the harm to their health by approving James's topic?

I'd promised an open mind. James was interested in an assignment, maybe for the first time in years. I took a deep breath, wondering what the school administration would say if they knew, and told him to go ahead. Hopefully, he wouldn't end his speech handing out chew like party favors.

When we went to the library, the librarian pulled me aside. "I haven't seen one of these kids in here before," he whispered. I smiled proudly, feeling like a mother duck leading her babies across a highway to water.

Several students changed topics when they couldn't find information to support their thesis. I hoped James would have that problem, but every time I saw him he had his head in a book or magazine, so he must have been finding what he needed. He could obviously read well when interested.

The day I asked who wanted to give his speech first, James's hand shot up.

"Go for it," I said.

James strode to the front of the class, a book in his hand, and took his place behind the podium. He pushed back blond hair that fell over one eye. "Man," he began, "you don't ever want to chew."

I leaned forward in my chair. Thankfully, he had changed his topic.

"If you chew, your teeth can fall out."

He waited, a natural orator, letting his audience take in what he'd said.

"It increases your heart rate and blood pressure. I don't want a heart attack."

Again he waited while the other students digested his words.

"The worst thing is, you can get cancer. You can lose your lip."

"Lose your lip?" a student squeaked.

"Think about it. You want half a lip? Who's going to kiss you if you have half a lip?" James pointed to his angular jaw. "Don't chew, man, the cancer can get your jaw or your neck. You won't ever get a date with part of your face gone."

One final time, he paused for his words to take root in everyone's minds.

"I'm never chewing again. The end."

The class sat stunned. "You're making it up," a student broke the silence.

James opened the book to a page of photos of oral cancer patients and showed it around.

"You're really quitting?" someone asked.

"You're crazy if you chew," he responded.

When James headed toward his seat, the class burst into applause. I clapped loudest of all. "Great job," I said. "You spoke clearly, you used your research well, and you kept your audience's attention. Best of all, you were willing to change your thesis based on the evidence you found. You have a really good mind to be able to do that."

"Are you saying I'm smart?" James sounded surprised.

"I'm saying you're *very* smart."

The class let out some hoots and wows and way-to-gos.

James's face turned red, and he smiled shyly.

I started planning my own persuasive speech. The thesis would be, "It's a gift to witness a student change his perception of himself and his life based on information he's discovered." I was going to enjoy teaching this class after all.

Not Everything is Black and White

by
Carol Commons-Brosowske

Hands down, my favorite and most challenging job ever involved working 12 years at an alternative high school. Lordy, I could write an entire book about the experiences I encountered. If cameras were allowed there, this place would have been a much better reality show than *Keeping Up with the Kardashians.*

I'll never forget my first day on the job—it was like entering a war zone. For one reason or another, these difficult teenagers had been expelled from their regular schools and placed into this one as a last stop before getting their "Go Directly to Jail" cards. Every student there was trouble with a capital "T." There were gang members, druggies and drug dealers. Attitudes were the worst I'd ever encountered, and their flipping the bird was everyday behavior.

This was my first job after being a stay-at-home mom for 18 years, and it was a scary place for this middle–aged housewife. As I walked through the front door of the school on that first day, two options ran through my mind: 1) Run for my life, never to return, or, 2) Go in with an attitude that I am strong and I can handle it. Fortunately, I chose the latter. Before the first week was over, I knew I'd found my niche. This was where I belonged. The staff quickly accepted me, and we became like family.

The building was an old grocery store that had been converted into a school. The space wasn't large, and you could hear every F-word bounce off the interior walls. Fights broke out on an hourly basis. A police officer was on duty at all times, trying to keep the peace.

I worked for the dean of students or, as the staff and I affectionately called him, "The Warden." This made me the warden's assistant. But the kids referred to the dean as "Coach," because he had coached football at his previous job. The Warden was a tall, good-looking black man with personality plus. His sense of humor made everyone's job fun, and he was a morale booster for staff and students. Plus, he had what it took to deal with the many sensitive situations he encountered.

My job description was to keep records on each student, including noting infractions and what actions had been taken, and I also worked directly with the truancy court system. Many times, numerous students were sent to us at the same time. My boss dealt directly with the worst offenders in his office. He was wonderful with them—patient, but firm. The kids loved and respected him, even if his punishment sometimes was harsh. I dealt with the ones who were sent to our office for minor offenses and attitude adjustments. Often, I considered putting up one of those number signs you see in the Department of Motor Vehicles: "Please take a number, have a seat and wait until your number is called." Other days, I'd rather have put a sign on the door stating: "Gone Fishing."

Another one of my job duties was to call the parents to inform them if their kids caused any incidents at school. I found out quickly that dealing with these out-of-control teens was a piece of cake compared to dealing with their parents. On the phone, I was called a "bitch," a "moron" and other names not suitable for polite print. My way of dealing with these types of parents was simply to hang up on them.

It didn't take long to learn that most of these kids were products of highly dysfunctional families. Sometimes these wayward teens just needed someone to listen, and that was my specialty. They shared with me things I'd had no clue existed except on the TV justice show *Nancy Grace*. I started out naïve. Before long, I felt comfortable handling most of these anxious students and their multitude of problems.

Besides parents calling staff members names, they swore to have us fired and made threats on a daily basis. Many lied to our faces—it was obvious they were angry and had no respect for themselves or others. They also wondered aloud how their kids could be the way they were. I told them, "The apple doesn't fall far from the tree."

I especially remember the day a16-year-old boy was caught with drugs. The city police were called to the school and were taking the child into custody. This time, Coach called the parents and got the student's mother on the other end. He put the call on speakerphone so that I could take notes.

Coach had never met this parent before. He introduced himself over the phone. She was pleasant enough at first, even though she didn't seem surprised or to care about the trouble her son was in for possession of drugs. She acted like it was a common thing. Then, all of a sudden, her attitude changed. She shouted loudly, "Shut up, nigger!"

I looked at my boss, and he looked at me. We both were horrified. The dean was nearly speechless, but being a true professional, he stammered into the phone, "Excuse me?"

"Oh, sorry," she explained, "the damn dog wouldn't stop barking."

After hanging up, the two of us shared a huge laugh. Can you imagine someone choosing such a horrible name for a dog?

Nearly every time I venture out these days, I run into one my old students. Many have turned their lives around. They always remember my name, and I always get a big hug. I did make a difference, something I had hoped for when I took that job working for the Warden.

The Warden and Carol

My First Day

by
Erin Blubaugh

After completing four years of college for my bachelor's degree, another year for my credentials, two quarters of student teaching and seven state exams, I was qualified to be a teacher. I was finally ready for my own classroom. Luckily, I scored a job at a Blue Ribbon college-prep high school in California that cranked out students bound for Ivy League colleges.

The morning of my first teaching assignment was surreal. I had totaled two hours of sleep the night before. As I entered the staff area, I was unsure on how to start a conversation with my new coworkers. So I blurted out, "Wow, bad idea to drink a whole pot of coffee on the first day of school, right?" In fact, I'd only had one cup, but I had to explain my jitters somehow. The faculty members responded to my comment with courteous laughter.

Now in my class, the morning bell finally rang. Within a matter of moments, I found 30-some pairs of eyes locked on me, judging, waiting for me to do my thing. *What am I supposed to be doing?!* I screamed inside my head. My mouth went dry. My hands shook. I wanted to forget the behavioral horrors of my last stint of student teaching, the one that explained why so many teachers avoided middle schools.

Luckily, my first class was a group of freshmen. They were as anxious about the first day of school as I was. They accepted me as their teacher simply because I was the adult at the front of the room. It was a relief that I wouldn't have to prove myself to this crowd.

I managed to get through my first three classes without sounding like a complete moron. In fact, I thought I sounded a little like a real teacher. Then along came fifth period, the class right after lunch. They were all juniors, and I would soon learn that, as upper classmen, they were well aware they ruled the school. I would have to play my coolness card—or, at least, fake it.

They filed in, yapping loudly with each other, enjoying inside jokes. *Are they laughing at me?* I felt better after checking that my fly was up. I directed them to their assigned seats, and once the last bell rang, I was on.

One kid wasn't sitting in his designated seat and was turned, with his back to me, engaged in conversation.

"Excuse me," I told him.

He turned and eyeballed me angrily. Evidently, I looked like a pushover, because he turned back around to resume his conversation.

God, how rude!

"I need you to take your seat up here," I said to him, pointing at his chair.

"What? I wasn't even talking," he said, lying.

Obviously, he was trying to start shit with me because I was a new teacher. This wasn't going to go well. Pointing out his lie would only cause more problems. Because I wasn't good with confrontation, it had been genius of me to pick teaching high school as a career. *Is Starbucks still hiring?* I wondered.

"You need to sit in *your* seat," I repeated. I gave my best serious-teacher look, trying to buy enough time to quickly review all my mental notes on classroom management 101. I knew if I didn't do this right, the Sweathogs would be taking over the rest of the year.

I decided to act tough. *Let him choose.*

"Look, you can sit here *or* in the office, I really don't care," I said.

My offer came across pretty convincingly to me. *What are the other kids thinking?* I wondered at the same time. I knew that scanning the room would make me look weak, as if I cared what the class thought. I took the stronger stance and kept my eyes pinned on him, ready for a showdown.

He stood up, moved to his seat and shut his pie hole. This sudden compliance startled me so that it took me a moment to remember the class lesson. I couldn't believe I had actually pulled it off!

The rest of the day went much smoother. For my last class, I would have freshmen, again. Since I'd had such a good experience with the first set of these creatures, I was certain it wouldn't be all that bad.

The freshmen filed in, took their assigned seats and seemed like a lively group. Lively, in the world of teaching, can mean either a gaggle of kids will be engaged and participate appropriately, or that it's time to start pre-writing the referral forms to the office. It turned out to be a strange mix of both, led by the Lord of the Flies, a character who loved nothing better than fart noises and peer laughter.

Luckily, the students didn't tie me up and light fire to the classroom on that first day, but I knew it was going to be an interesting year. Could you write a referral for burping out the teacher's name? After all, I couldn't tell if he was trying to call me "Mrs. Blue-balls" or if it just sounded that way.

Driving home, I was exhausted—but I had survived! The first day was over, and I had made it. All that preparation. All that expectation and worry. I felt as if I could go home and sleep for a week.

As I sat in bumper-to-bumper traffic thinking of what to make for dinner, it hit me. I still had to go back the next day!

School Daze

by
Erika Hoffman

I wish there was one special student who stood out above all the rest or that I was that teacher who made a difference in a kid's life. In reality, my 10 years of teaching are a kaleidoscope blur, like a fast merry-go-round of sights and sounds with intermittent bouts of nausea.

Often, the names and faces I glimpse in my mind's eye belong to the class clowns, the troublemakers, future felons, wannabe ax murderers . . . that type. I recall those best who most resembled enemy combatants on the front lines. Sure, sweet kids existed who did their best, obeyed as told and learned, but those names and visages slip from a teacher's corroded memory. It's the Jesse James of the schoolmarm's wild, wild room that she remembers. It's the snarling faces, the sagging pants and the defiant tone she can't forget.

One supercilious fellow—a varsity baseball pitcher who

skipped class routinely—comes to mind. I made him miss practice and serve detention with me during which I lectured him on his lack of priorities. "Someday, you'll find it more important to understand the difference between transitive and intransitive verbs than to play silly ballgames." Later, those words ricocheted back to haunt me. That boy made millions as a pitcher in the major leagues!

Unfortunately, I suffered from chronic foot-in-mouth disease. On top of that, I was a running slapstick comedy. When I was 22, I used to collect souvenir matchboxes. I'd toss them in my overstuffed bag with all the other junk I, the packrat, had gathered. One day, I threw my bag hard on my desk after some student made a snide crack about the reading assignment, *Bartleby*. I strode over to the lectern and pontificated on the theme of social welfare as evidenced in Melville's tale. Trying to elicit a response from a sea of glazed eyes, I was stunned at the sudden perkiness of my students who began waving frantically, pointing and laughing. "Miss Vogel, your purse is on fire!" a joker yelled out.

"April Fool's Day was yesterday. We had our little fun then, remember? Today's April 2nd; time for work," I replied smugly. I heard a crackling behind me. I smelled burning hair. I glanced back. Rising smoke issued from my chimney of a pocketbook! Somehow, the matches had struck each other, igniting calling cards, menus, tissue, my hairbrush and all things flammable hoarded in my bulging bag. I shoved it onto the floor and stomped on it, which was a crowd-pleasing stunt. That was the only day all year 100 percent of my students paid attention.

For a spell, I mimicked a "cool" teacher and sat pretty on my desk with ankles demurely crossed. Being short, I had to hop down rather than step down gracefully. Since I'm always absent-minded and often clueless, I paid no attention to where the janitor placed the trashcan each night. One evening, he put it right under my desk. The next morning, I was yakking on and on about some metaphor and never looked before I leaped . . . into it. It tumbled over, and I fell out—*splat!*—much to the amusement of the masses.

In one North Carolina school in the late 1970s, before air conditioning was installed, we had ancient, heavy windows. During the dog days of September, I tried to lift one. The window plunged, catching my pointer finger with its metal casement. I saw stars. I thought I'd vomit in front of my audience. I staggered to my desk like a happy-hour drunk and passed out, my head in bloody hands. Before I knew it, the bell was ringing and class was over. To this day, I have no idea what the kids did while I was out of it for those 20 minutes, but I didn't hear a sound.

Another unforgettable episode was when I was 23. This Georgia high school gave us an hour-long lunch break, but no teacher was supposed to leave campus. I'd fallen in love with the Burger King Whopper. So my gal pal—the art teacher—and I sneaked down the road to satisfy our craving for what then was an exciting new sandwich. Trouble is, my Celica ST stalled out. We had to return before our next class resumed, so we hitchhiked back with guys in a pickup who were doppelgangers for misfits in a Stephen King thriller. After that, my fellow aficionado of Whoppers refused to do lunch with me.

I did more stupid things than just these few recalled and recorded. I did countless more asinine things than the teens I taught. My memory has graciously allowed me to forget some to save me from remembering what a dope I was. Yet, one persistent memory pops to mind, unsuppressed all these years though I've tried to bury it.

I had to write a pass for a nervous young man to see his counselor about something or other. I was always harried, tired and spacey in my 20s. I reached down into my gargantuan sack to grab a thick pen, which I did. I then began pressing down hard with the pen onto the official pinkish pass slip, but the pen wouldn't write. The boy gazed hard at my script. I shook the pen. Nothing.

When I glanced up at him, his eyes widened. I followed his steadfast gaze at the pen between my fingers. My pen wasn't a pen at all. The wrapper was frayed, and protruding from it was a white, thick tampon. I froze, speechless. The teen stared at me. I turned red. He turned redder. I don't recall much after that.

There were also the fun encounters with the "involved" parents. Once I told unruly seventh-grade kids in North Carolina I was going to use the carrot and stick approach in the classroom. Before 24 hours had passed, a mother called the school principal, claiming I threatened to beat kids with sticks. Another time, a student asked me for a title suggestion for a seventh-grade newspaper she wanted to produce to spill the gossip of her girls' group. I suggested the name, *The Scuttlebutt.* Yup! A mama phoned my boss—she didn't think any anatomy parts should be talked about in a school newspaper, especially large backsides.

When I think of my "school daze," I marvel that work got done in spite of numerous interruptions by the loudspeaker, fire drills, tornado drills, impromptu pep rallies and scheduled events, and that discipline was maintained despite the bucking bronco stance of some students and their parents. Usually, the entire classroom kept an ambiance of enthusiasm no matter how tedious the material could be. We had our fun . . . even if it came at the expense of an Amelia Bedelia-type teacher whose goofy snafus and unsolicited advice often missed the mark. I didn't resemble that stellar pedagogue of yore from the book and movie *Goodbye, Mr. Chips*. Or the one Robin Williams portrayed in *Dead Poets Society*. I was closer to the type Cameron Diaz immortalized. What was the name of that movie? *Bad Teacher!*

Learning to Fly High

by
John J. Lesjack

Back in my first years of classroom teaching, my science program involved the study of the French-born Montgolfier brothers and their first hot air balloons. My students thought the subject matter quirky yet perfect for the creative instincts of their fifth-grade abilities. They were excited about working in teams to construct and launch hot air balloons, 8 feet tall, made out of tissue paper. Teachers had academic freedom back then and often used Einstein's quote, "Imagination is more important than knowledge."

I got along well with students and their parents, who quickly supported my teachings and our latest topic and project. One parent created a functional "launching pot" out of a metal 5-gallon can with a stovepipe on top. An opening near the bottom allowed crumpled newspapers to be inserted where they burned safely, the heat channeling upward as a warm air thermal. And students happily took on jobs within their teams—pilot, chase crew, timer and recorder of the flight log, despite being disappointed that our balloons would carry no passengers. "That's been done already," I explained in front of the whole class. "We'll do something with longer-reaching implications."

In the lesson, the pilot held a balloon above the stovepipe while a parent hooked a stick in the string at the top of the balloon. Another parent served as fireman. The pilot used the Montgoflier-originated command, "Hand's off!" and released the inflated aircraft. The timer set the stopwatch to ticking and deployed the chase crew—two students—to track the balloon. A record keeper, who wrote the balloon's name and flight number in the flight log, also wrote about its time aloft.

Smiling Bobby Pierre provided a happy memory. Bobby loved the color green, so he traded for extra sheets of green tissue paper in order to concoct a huge balloon. As he said, "A big balloon flies higher." He also loved using Scotch tape. On launch day, Bobby-the-pilot carried his balloon, called "Pierre's Pickle," onto the playground. He swirled the balloon around to fill it with air then held it over the launching pot. Warm air flowed. Bobby's crew waited. The fireman added more fuel. Slowly, Pierre's Pickle inflated. Finally, Bobby yelled, "Hands off!"

Struggling to get airborne, Pierre's Pickle drifted away from the launching pot, landed on the ground and collapsed. Students laughed and shouted, "You used too much tape!"

Bobby laughed, too, as he said, "It ain't easy being green."

During my second year of ballooning, multicolored patchwork-quilt patterns were popular, but a blue dome with red and white stripes and a ballast covered with white stars led all designs. The exception was Athena Olson's unforgettable doughnut-shaped "UFO."

Athena's crew used white tissue paper, complete with little round pieces of aluminum foil, to imitate windows. Our balloons made no sound, but their silent presence sometimes startled people, caused horses to gallop and dogs to bark. Once released, Athena's dramatic creation rose about 200 feet above the schoolyard and drifted down near the fence where she waited. Suddenly, a frightened woman appeared on the sidewalk, frantically pushing a baby buggy.

Through the fence, Athena shouted, "Where are you going, Mom?"

"Home to call the fire department to report a UFO! Come on home with me now, Athena."

When Athena grabbed the tissue paper UFO, her mother nearly passed out. Athena waved to the record keeper then turned to her mother and said, "Mom, I made this in class. It's part of our hot air balloon unit."

All of our flights were untethered and launched during windless early mornings in Northern California. If we flew after the winds came up, the balloons would blow off school grounds, landing on rooftops. They would get caught in trees or sail across the highway, in which case traffic would have to stop.

One afternoon, before the last school bell rang, I advised my students to check treetops on their way to school in the morning. If the treetops were not moving, conditions would be perfect for our first adventure of the school year.

Marvelous morning weather excited the students, who ripped one balloon while carrying it across the playground. We taped our second balloon wrong, and it refused to hold hot air. Then, five balloons soared high above the playground in spectacular fashion—three in the air at the same time— averaging two minutes flying time each, and we successfully retrieved them. The next balloon rode an air current out into the neighborhood, landing in a swimming pool where it dyed the water purple.

Our last balloon rose 250 feet, drifted in a southwest current and was last seen above Heavenly Hamburger down the highway. Because its chase crew, which was not allowed to cross streets or climb fences, was disappointed at the loss, I said, "My experience tells me that your balloon will come back in ways we can't imagine."

Before we had put our ballooning gear away, two tall, serious-looking policemen showed up in my classroom. "You the guy launching hot air balloons?" the first cop asked.

"I was," I confessed as I hung up a balloon that reeked of smoke.

The second cop pointed to the balloon. "Is this what you launched?"

"It is."

"Did one of these fly over Heavenly Hamburger?"

"It did."

"Where's the basket?"

"No basket," I said. "Tissue paper has barely enough lift

to get itself off the ground. Am I in trouble?"

The cop spoke into his walkie-talkie and instructed, "Call off the helicopter." Both cops ducked their heads and walked out of my classroom, just before the reporter and the photographer entered. My students were in a state of awe. As the photographer took pictures, the reporter filled me in on the morning's news.

About 8 A.M., city police got reports that the basket of a balloon, obviously containing a person, had snapped off and had fallen to the ground, from 500 feet in the sky, in the Spring Lake Park area. It was reported that a volunteer at the nearby fire station saw a hot air balloon above Heavenly Hamburger shortly after 8:30 A.M. and sounded the alarm.

City authorities then launched—no pun intended— a full-scale search for the collapsed balloon, its basket and its passengers. Police and fire department rescuers, with the news media close behind, searched the park. During a hectic 45-minute search, dispatchers called all public facilities and, just minutes before the sheriff's department helicopter cranked up, the police dispatcher contacted my school secretary.

"I've been doing this for years," I told the reporter. "I've competed with other schools and their hot air balloons. I've been on television and in the local newspapers, but none of my flights ever attracted much attention."

What happened was that our last balloon ascended, drifted south and found the restaurant's chimney. The innocent balloon, trapped by the thermal from the restaurant's broiler, soared to about 300 feet and hung in the air above

Heavenly Hamburger, unmoving, for several minutes. Seen from a distance, our 8-foot replica looked like a real 80-foot tall commercial hot air balloon . . . minus a basket.

We just proved that warm air rises and, in rising, has lift. And we imitated the Montgolfier brothers, who first launched paper balloons in France in 1782. But, more specifically, we improved on the Frenchmen's theory. They thought smoke made a balloon rise. My fifth-graders proved warm air lifted the balloons.

The next day, our story and picture were on the front page of the local newspaper: BALLOON PLUNGE A BIG LESSON. A day later, the fire department informed me of a new ordinance that said any open fires on school grounds required a $10 permit.

Teacher John holds the balloon steady while his students and a parent fill it with hot air.

Losing My Innocence in High School

by
Chris Stansbury

Being an educational assistant for the special education department was rewarding and interesting—but often challenging, too. "Never a dull moment" is a term that comes to mind as I remember the students and staff I encountered over the years.

In the beginning, I was at the grade-school level, teaching small groups of students who needed extra attention in reading, writing, math and life skills. The younger children were eager to learn and excited about their accomplishments, but they were still innocent and naïve about many things. It seems that I was, too.

The most risqué it ever got was when a fifth-grade student snickered uncontrollably as he read the sentence, "Joe has blue balls," in a first-grade-level reading book. Honestly, I don't know what the author was thinking!

My transition to the high-school level came in December. One day while I walked to lunch, the principal called me into her office. Her serious demeanor made me feel apprehensive about the meeting. "We need both a teacher and an assistant to move to the high school by the first of the year," she said, "and we would like you to be that assistant. Will you go?"

Immediately, I felt sweaty and nervous. High school students were big. They kind of scared me. This position was way out of my comfort zone. The principal then told me that the teacher who had accepted the teaching position was the person who had mentored me. That made me feel better, and I agreed to the transfer. Two weeks later, the two of us began work at the new school.

Just as I expected, the students were larger, most of them much taller than my 5-feet 2-inches. After having struggled for years with their learning disabilities, many of the students seemed less eager to learn by the time they reached high school. In some ways, they seemed to be maturing, but at the same time, they were hormonal and sometimes moody. I found, however, that I could talk to them as adults. I loved that they understood my sense of humor, even if I didn't always understand theirs.

The first time it hit me that I had entered a new world was the day a young teenage girl came and sat at my desk. She seemed worried and nervous. I encouraged her to talk, and soon she said quietly, with tears in her eyes, "I think I have an STD."

I was familiar with STP motor oil, but I had no idea

what an STD was, and I was pretty sure it had nothing to do with maintaining an automobile. "What's an STD?" I asked. She looked at me as if I were stupid. Her expression said, "Duh!" as she replied, "It's a sexually transmitted disease." My innocent days at the high school had officially ended.

The next fall, as the leaves turned orange, brown and yellow and the air felt cool and crisp, the excitement of homecoming week surrounded us. The homecoming court had been chosen, the football players were getting ready for the big game and many students busily prepared for the festivities.

One morning during first period, a freshman girl excitedly entered the classroom. This was her first homecoming and she couldn't wait to decorate for the celebration. Soon she gathered large pieces of yellow butcher paper and many permanent markers and started making posters. She was enraptured with the project, and I loved watching her put positive energy into showing school spirit.

Our classroom had a wall of windows facing the walkway between two buildings, a perfect place to hang signs. Everyone would see the bright signs the girl was making to support the school sports team—the Lions. Masking tape in hand, she posted two large signs in the window. Her big grin showed that she felt extremely proud of herself, and I was proud of her, too. It was fabulous having the class participate in homecoming.

The bell rang. Laughter and conversation filled the hallway as students went to their next classes. Suddenly, a male student rushed into the classroom. "Those yellow signs look good," he said, "but I think you'd better check the spelling!"

Immediately, I went to check. Sure enough, the girl had misspelled one of the words. The signs read, "*Loins* Rock!" and "Go *Loins*!"

Of course, "lions" and "loins" are two entirely different things. I knew that students, with raging teenage hormones, were heading over from the other building and these messages were not the ones we wanted to send. So I tore down the signs . . . fast!

Along with losing my innocence by learning about STDs, I had learned to proofread everything.

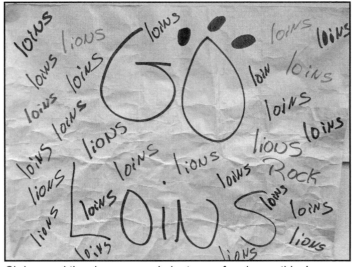

Chris saved the sign as a reminder to proofread everything!

A Piece of Cake

by
Ken McKowen

When I retired after 30 years with the California State Park System, I decided to try substitute teaching at our local public elementary school. After all, I had taught adults everything from police defensive tactics, CPR and advanced first aid to grant writing, photography and writing, so how difficult could it be to teach a classroom full of kids? And besides, my wife Dahlynn and I had been volunteering at the same school for several years.

One of my first assignments was teaching a second grade class for two weeks. The regular teacher was having surgery, but was creating the daily lesson plans, so I figured the assignment would be a piece of cake—and fun! Plus, the extra money would be nice, too.

The first week went by reasonably well. I got to know the kids and quickly understood why two students had their seats in the back of the room, away from everyone else. A student, who sat near the front, was constantly crawling underneath his desk. Not to be outdone, another student turned out to be a drama queen and became overexcited about everything—she was forever bouncing up and down out of her seat. The star pupil of the class was actually a first-grader who had been moved up to the second grade. He was academically way ahead of most of the second graders and was always the first to finish his in-class assignments.

On the last day of subbing for the class, it happened to be Angel's birthday. Angel was one of the two students sitting by themselves in the back of the class. Angel was not a well-chosen name for this child. She was constantly out of her seat, talking nonstop and being disruptive. When I spent one-on-one time with her, Angel was quite bright and creative, but not inclined to adapt to anyone else's priorities.

Angel's mother brought in three packages of those fancy store-bought, piled-high-with-frosting cupcakes so the class could celebrate her daughter's birthday. The students were excited about the party, but I told them we would wait until the end of the day to sing *Happy Birthday* and share Angel's cupcakes. They were disappointed, but pretended to understand that we had to stay focused on the day's assignments.

Finally, with 20 minutes left in the school day, I asked an instructional aide to begin passing out the cupcakes. That's when I looked down and saw my desk-diver kid under his desk for the zillionth time that day, but this time, there was a substantial amount of blood running down his face. I quickly pulled him out from under his desk and slapped a wet paper towel on his wound to get the bleeding under control. Leaving the aide in charge for a few minutes, I took the boy immediately to the office. When I returned, I looked under the desk and saw an exposed bolt had been the culprit.

With now only 10 minutes left, my bouncing Betty jumped up from her seat once again, right when the aide was getting ready to give her a cupcake. Betty's head connected with the open plastic package of cupcakes and sent them flying across the room, landing frosting side down onto the classroom's carpet.

As I was cleaning up that mess, the aide grabbed another package and continued passing out more cupcakes. That's when my genius first grader walked over and excitedly showed me the chocolate frosting he had smeared over his entire face. "I'm going to show my mommy I had a chocolate cupcake," he proudly informed me.

Trying to decide whether or not to clean Einstein up before his mom saw him, I noticed another student giving the international choking sign—he had his hands at his throat and was quickly turning a nice shade of blue. I grabbed him, slapped him on the back a few times then had to resort to a quick thrust to his stomach. Out shot what appeared to be an entire cupcake, which had been partially chewed. With him breathing again, the bell thankfully rang and I quickly dismissed the class, but not before escorting the boy who had choked to the office.

I never did get one of those cupcakes for myself, but I will admit, I did have a few glasses of wine when I got home.

The Biology Lesson

by
Laurel McHargue

"Oh, Miss? Could you tell me what is an 'orgasm'?"

Starting the first hour of the day with my small class of 10th grade English Language Learners was always a challenge, but I loved the fact that my students felt they could ask me anything. This was not the first time that an unexpected question had arisen, and I was quite certain it would not be the last. The challenge, I always discovered, was in answering the question in a way that was professional, accurate and respectful. There were no "stupid questions" in my classroom. Still, a question of this nature required extra thoughtfulness before answering.

"What assignment are you working on?" I deflected, buying myself time to consider my response. At the start of each class, I would give my students about 20 minutes to do work from other classes, and that gave me an opportunity to work on their academic language skills.

"Biology. They were talking about it in this film, but I didn't get it."

"OK. Well, let's start with the dictionary then. No, not the abridged version . . . get the big one." *Let Webster do the work*, I thought. *Can't go wrong there.*

"How you spell it? O . . . R . . . G . . ." she began.

"A . . . S . . . M," I finished for her, happy to assist with dictionary-search techniques, too. I would turn this into a multi-genre lesson, and everyone would learn more than they had anticipated.

The problem with Webster, however, is that definitions are sometimes complex, and especially with new-language learners, require the student to look up other words within the definition.

"Intense or paro . . . what? Paroxysmal—what is that?— excitement? I don't get this, Miss. This is stupid."

Hell, even I didn't know what Webster was saying, and I'd been enjoying orgasms in this English-speaking country for decades. I knew that if I hoped to accomplish the day's English lesson, I would have to intervene and provide my own explanation. I would do my best to keep it relevant to the reproductive cycle I assumed they were discussing in biology class.

My students listened with rapt attention as I provided the basics of the physical "climax," a word we would later discuss when talking about the elements of a short story. I added humor when I explained the differences between a male and a female orgasm. After all, my understanding of the other was purely secondhand!

When I finished my explanation, I was surprised that there were no follow-on questions, and my students seemed overly ready to begin their English lesson. Typically, they would welcome a sidetrack from the daily grind. *Good!* I thought. *I responded appropriately and in terminology my students will understand and remember should there be a test.*

Several weeks later I shared my story at the dinner table with some teacher friends, my husband and my sons, the youngest who had recently graduated from our high school. I wanted them to know the kinds of issues I dealt with on a daily basis . . . and I really wanted them to know what a cool teacher I was that I could answer such questions without missing a beat.

"Ahhhhh, Mom? Do you think maybe they were asking you what an 'organism' is?" my youngest asked, starting to snicker.

Oh. My. God. That would explain so much.

The entire table erupted in laughter as I became the target of good-natured ridicule, but I tried to stick to my guns. Surely, they could have heard "orgasm" in a biology film! I reminded my oldest son that he had learned all about "nocturnal ejaculations" in sixth grade but had no idea what that meant. Surely I had not misunderstood my student!

"But Mom, they're just learning English! And we did NOT learn about orgasms in 10th grade biology," insisted my son.

By this time most of us—including myself—had tears in our eyes as we took turns trying to imagine what must have been going through my students' heads during my "lesson."

The next morning I rushed to the biology class before the morning bell, certain that several of my students had gotten into trouble—because of me—for their answers on a test. Once the biology teacher stopped laughing, she told me that there had been no test on the film about "organisms."

I'll never know why my explanation to my ESL students that day did not result in more questions, but I'm fairly certain that they were able to share some laughter around their own dinner tables as they recounted the multi-genre biology lesson taught by their English teacher.

CHAPTER THREE

Human Resources

Relationships in the workplace . . .

On the Prowl

by
Bobby Barbara Smith

"I'll get this one!" I pushed past the counter girls like a charging lion after its prey.

The man walking in the door was a regular customer at the high-end dry cleaners where I worked as front manager. I was a divorced mother of three with no time and no interest in dating. But this guy intrigued me. He had a way of looking me straight in the eye, with his head slightly tilted. And oh, those eyes . . . the most gorgeous blue eyes I'd ever seen! He had my attention, but I knew he had a live-in girlfriend. I was not one to infringe on a happy relationship, but were they really happy? Some days, he seemed so sad.

Most of my duties at the dry cleaners took place behind the partitioned wall, training new counter personnel, handling customer complaints and making sure things ran smoothly.

Frequently, my counter girls waited on customers at the front counter, but whenever I spotted Mr. Blue Eyes coming in, I made a beeline to the front, tripping any foolish counter girl who dared to cross my path.

Then came the day when the live-in girlfriend, who also had her dry cleaning done by our store, supplied us with her new address. Hot damn! I scurried behind the partition and literally did a happy dance while my counter girls looked on in disbelief. I even surprised myself. *What on earth are you thinking? You don't have time for this,* I scolded myself, but I couldn't shake the excitement building inside me.

The next day, Mr. Blue Eyes came in with a smile as big as Texas and a spring in his step. Just then, the lobby filled with customers, which didn't allow time for chit-chat. Where were my ever-so-helpful counter girls? My frustration escalated.

"Hello! I could use some help up front!" I hollered toward the back room.

I knew he wanted to ask me out, if given a chance, and I wanted to give him that chance. But a lobby full of people didn't lend a proper setting to ask one out on a date. He left, and I pouted.

One day, he dropped off a suit jacket, and immediately the lobby filled with customers. I selected the "clean and press" box on his ticket and could do nothing but watch as he made his way out the door.

"Help up front, please," I growled, and counter girls scurried around the partition. I sniffed the lingering scent of cologne on his jacket and stared at his ticket.

I have his name and address, so all I need is his phone number, I thought. My hands trembled with excitement as I thumbed through the phone book, and the excitement mounted as I ran my finger down the list to his number. "Voila!" I rushed to the phone before my logical left-brain could stop me.

When he answered, I stammered then plunged forward at full throttle. "I forgot if you wanted your suit jacket cleaned or just pressed." My nose grew longer as I spun my web.

Mr. Blue Eyes didn't waste any time seizing the opportunity. "I'm glad you called. I wonder if you'd have lunch with me, that is, if you're not in a relationship." He paused, and my heart did a flip-flop.

"Oh, no . . . I mean, no, I'm not in a relationship. I'd love to have lunch." I was positively giddy as I hung up.

The following Monday, we had lunch and every day until the weekend. He learned from our conversations that I had three children and that weekends were the only time I had with them. But he had a plan. "How about I come over and help you with that yardwork?"

My left brain told me to say, "No," but my right brain remained lost in those blue eyes. I pulled back out of my trance. "I couldn't ask you to do that."

"You didn't ask, I volunteered. I love yard work," he said. "That's the one thing I hate about living in an apartment. I have no yard. Besides," he continued, "there's something I love even more than yardwork, and that's spending time with you!"

Gulp! How could I say no?

I rarely brought dates to my house. I didn't want to add stress to my children's lives, but Mr. Blue Eyes waltzed right in . . . mowing grass, spending his days off with me and the kids then driving back to his apartment at night. This mama led by example. There was no hanky-panky allowed under my roof.

As we found more and more things we had in common, we became completely enraptured. I was falling for this blue-eyed charmer, and he wasn't letting any grass grow as he expressed his love and intentions to marry me.

As crazy as I was about this guy, I was in the process of moving my aging mother in with me. "I can't even begin to think about marriage now. I have no idea how this is going to work out with Mom. You must be crazy, wanting to take on a ready-made-family AND a live-in mother-in-law!" I shook my head in disbelief.

"I'll do whatever it takes to make you mine." His blue eyes twinkled, but I stood my ground. I could not bring him into this three-ring-circus; it wouldn't be fair.

So I moved Mom in, and Mr. Blue Eyes proceeded to charm her, too. "He looks a little like Clark Gable," she quipped as she watched him mowing the grass. "He's a good man, Bobby."

"I know, Mom, I know."

One Friday night as I rushed home from work, I made a mental list of what I'd fix for dinner, and I hoped I'd have time to do the dishes before my man arrived. I was bone tired as I pulled into the drive. *Oh crud, he beat me here! Could this day get any worse?*

The aroma of food cooking greeted me as I opened the door. I stood on the landing for a moment, thinking I must be in the wrong house. Then, looking up the stairs, I saw the most amazing thing. Mr. Blue Eyes stood at my kitchen sink washing my dirty dishes. On the stove was an array of pots, steaming with food.

As he turned to greet me, I said the first thing that popped into my head. "I can't believe what I'm seeing! Will you marry me?" I chuckled at my joke, thinking I was clever. A man washing my dirty dishes was the sexiest thing I could imagine.

"Yes! Yes, I will marry you! And I have witnesses, so you can't wiggle out of this one." He pointed across the room. His witnesses—my mom and my daughter—grinned from ear to ear.

So that's how I became Mrs. Blue Eyes, and that joke was the best joke I ever told. He can't say I "took him to the cleaners," but I can tell everyone that's where I found him.

Bobby at the dry cleaners (right) and on their wedding day

All's Fair in Love

by
Sioux Roslawski

I looked fetching in my polyester dress. Part of the allure was due to the garish color combination—lemon yellow and red—and part of the sex appeal of my outfit was because splotches of ketchup and grease almost always embellished the front.

I was a waitress. I was a single mother. I was also a divorcee, and I was on the prowl for a new significant other.

The guys that came in every morning and sat at the counter, sucking up cheap coffee for an hour or more, did not appeal to me. One of them worked with horses. I loved horses. Unfortunately, I didn't love men who smelled like what came out of the rear end of horses. Another one of the guys had a loud, braying laugh. Like a donkey. And to add to the ass similarity, he laughed. Often. At his own jokes—jokes that weren't funny.

The rest of the male customers were also unappealing,

for various reasons. Since none of them were prospects filled with promise, I set my sights on another employee in the restaurant—the assistant manager.

Why him? It wasn't because he earned a big salary, that's for sure! This restaurant was an equal opportunity user and abuser—everyone's paychecks were anorexic, and everyone was overworked. It also wasn't because he was a charming conversationalist. This guy got tongue-tied every time I scurried up to the cook's line to turn in a ticket. He'd be in front of the grill helping the cook get the orders out while I'd be leaning over the counter to finish writing out the order, the neckline of my polyester uniform gaping open, and . . .

Maybe that's why he was rendered speechless every time I got near him, why he'd sometimes blush when I approached him. Whatever the reason, we soon began a workplace romance. Although ours was a strange form of flirtation, there were sparks nonetheless. We played jokes on each other.

For example, my guy—the assistant manager—and his boss—the manager—always held their weekly meeting over lunch. Invariably, my beau would choose for them to be seated in my section. Not only did that mean no tip from that table, but it also meant I would have to run back and forth because of his idiotic requests.

"And I'd like small onion rings with that sandwich. Only small ones." His eyebrows arched up mischievously when he gave me his order. After fuming inside, I'd have to go into the walk-in freezer and handpick tiny onion rings for the cook to fry up. What a pain. He wanted ice in his soda. Lots of ice. I'd have to make several trips getting just the right amount of ice in his glass.

My boyfriend also slammed me with customers. I was not the most efficient of servers. In fact, I was quite flighty and distracted as I raced around the dining room, dropping off full plates and picking up empty ones. Good cooks will help servers out by timing when the orders come out. Cooks who care will make sure there is some time between the orders so the waitperson can deliver a table's food and have time to come back to the servers' counter before the next order is ready. I was not so lucky. My assistant-manager-turned-boyfriend conspired with the cook to ensure that all my orders were ready—at the same time.

Brrrring! "Sioux, table four's food is up."

Brrrring! "Sioux, your order's ready and under the warmer."

Brrrring! "Sioux, pick up your food. It's getting cold."

Looking over the warming counter that was full of more than a dozen plates—all for my diners—I'd see him. With a wink and a smirk, he'd leave the kitchen and head to the office, where he was safe from my ranting and raving.

Knowing that revenge is a dish best served cold, I was hot on his trail to get even. After much thought, I created the perfect scheme.

Finding the number of an adult toy store in the phone book, I called. I explained what I was looking for, and they said they had several in stock.

"What color of hair?" the clerk asked.

"I don't know. Red?"

"Extra-strength plastic or standard?"

Gulp. "Standard strength is fine, I guess."

"An anatomically correct model?"

Shudder. *Eeeew.* "Yes."

Ending the conversation as quickly as possible, I headed to the store, which was in a sketchy part of town. Looking around the parking lot to make sure no one was able to spot me, I pulled the hood of my jacket up to hide my face and slipped into the store. As soon as I crossed the threshold, the words tumbled out.

"I called earlier about the blow-up doll. It's a joke. It's not for me. I'm pulling a prank on someone." The guy at the cash register couldn't have cared less, and I imagine he'd heard the it's-not-for-me-it's-for-a-friend excuse many times before. After reminding him of what I wanted, he shuffled back to the stockroom and returned with a good-sized and surprisingly heavy package.

To prepare my giggle-inducing gag gift, I dressed her in one of my waitress uniforms. Her mouth was wide-open—and it horrified me there was a pouch in place so things could be inserted into that big mouth of hers. To make matters worse, her mouth wasn't the only thing that was wide-open. Once I got her dressed, I blew her up—and when she was full of my hot breath, her legs sprang open to form a wide, upside-down "V." It was disgusting and hilarious at the same time.

Putting the finishing touches on my attempt at payback, I wrapped her in plain brown paper, making sure her legs were pulled together in a chaste way, and asked my brother to deliver her to my boyfriend at the restaurant. My little brother dressed up in the uniform he wore when he worked as a mechanic at a local garage—as I requested—and he brought along a clipboard to look even more official.

When the package was opened—in the kitchen in front of the cook—and the doll's legs sprang open, my sweetie's face turned as red as ketchup. I was taking an order on the other side of the dining room when it happened, but I made sure to pause so I could drink in his reaction.

Our eyes met, and we both knew without a shred of doubt that I had won the battle. Victory was mine, at least for that moment.

Eventually, I moved on to another job. He did, too, and yet, 27 years later, we're still laughing and still pulling pranks on each other. We're parents and grandparents, and thankfully, the spark has never disappeared.

My Tribe

by
Staci Lawrence

My sister Sarah and I grew up in a modest brick home in a Detroit suburb. My dad, David, worked for an automaker. My mom, Joan, hauled Sarah and me to school functions, dance lessons and play rehearsals. Our parents supported us, always encouraging us to believe in our dreams. Mine was to be an actress and a dancer.

My husband, Dax, and I live in California, far away from my childhood home. My parents died before I became a mother, and I miss their loving support. When our first daughter, Isla, was just one month old, I wrote in my journal, "Dax and I are thinking of hiring a mommy's helper . . . just for a couple of hours a day, just to help us keep balance." I laugh at that now because little did I know that my company, Flash Mob America, was about to explode.

Up until that time, we had been doing great. As the

world's first and largest flash mob production company, we had fans all over the world, participants and producers all over the country. We had appeared on *Modern Family*, the *Rachael Ray* show and the series finale of *Kimora: Life in the Fab Lane* and had a steady but manageable stream of corporate gigs. We had never once solicited business, and judging by the thousands of unmanageable inquiries we received, things were ramping up.

By the time Isla was four months old, Dax and I had the support of a full-time nanny and a pre-production staff of three. We had been thrown into a joy-filled whirlwind as we simultaneously became new parents and opened our home to FMA. Our lives suddenly went from quietly working alongside each other in our little home office to sharing our entire home with our new baby and a staff of people who worked late into the night. And it was awesome. Life became a sitcom.

Akil—Isla's "Manny" and my personal assistant—is a cross-dressing Gypsy. He has three addresses, doesn't pay rent where he stays and has all his meals and transportation taken care of. He has dreadlocks decorated with African beads and was raised Muslim, but is now a Buddhist. He is hilarious, was a child actor on Broadway and loves our daughter as his own.

Recently, I looked around our dining room table at these people who are now part of our tribe, this village of influence for our daughter. Another staffer—Chris—is a self-proclaimed control-freak culinary grad with a snobby persona masking a very big heart. He's a great cook and prepares lunch for our staff and dinner for our family every day he comes in. He's so awesome at his job that I resent him for having other dreams, though I am 100 percent supportive when he leaves for months at a time to create food porn on reality TV.

Lunch conversations usually center on whether or not something is racist or gay. Chris explained that he always says, "Drive forward" instead of "Drive straight," and we discussed whether that's a political stance or just simply gay. Dax asked how he explains "straightforward."

My heart warmed as I took a silent moment of gratitude for Isla's playmates who are with her when I cannot be. These playmates do funny things with her, like wear tutus on their heads, dance to every genre of music and practice yoga and tai chi in the living room wearing beads in their dreads and spiked earrings in their ears. They feed Isla organic home-made food and let her get soaking wet in the backyard. They follow her every request and walk her around the neighborhood, explaining airplanes and birds, doggies and ducks. She loves her iPad, her Wheely Bug and her purse, and of course, Mommy's underwear *must* be worn on her head.

Tonight, as I rushed to leave the house for acting class, it occurred to me that I had forgotten dinner. *Gasp!* "Where's my lemon pound cake? I didn't eat dinner!"

Akil snapped to and slid across the living room in his socks, rushing to grab the cake.

"Wait! I need my headset!"

Chris called out from the kitchen, where he was making Isla's dinner, "It's in your office, right next to your computer, underneath the papers and the calculator, on the left!"

Dax asked, "Do you want a bar or something?" as he strapped Isla into her high chair. She was oblivious to my leaving, content with the tribe, the people bustling around her who made it possible for me to do this type of work.

Akil had an idea. "Almonds!" He rushed to get them. I jiggled my phone, headset, wallet, keys and random piles of food.

Chris called out, "You want some salami?!"

"Yes!" He handed me a pile of salami. In a hurry, I rushed around kissing cheeks: Isla, Dax, Chris, Akil. "Love you. Love you. Thank you. Love you. Thank you. Love you."

As I opened the door and stepped onto the porch, Dax said in his medieval storyteller voice, "Will there be anything else, your highness?" Everyone laughed, and I called out, "No, that will be all, thank you." I heard, "Drive safe!" as the door closed.

Jumping into my Volvo, I dumped my random snacks onto the passenger seat then turned the key. The radio played *Dance All Night* by Poison Clan. That would be from high school. I was struck by the time warp; high school music blaring from my Volvo as I drove away from my tribe, my husband and our two multicultural gay assistants, all three of them focused on feeding our baby because the boobs had just driven away.

I'd spent so many years leading up to that moment, dreaming about gaining visibility as an actress while, at the same time, dreaming of having a family. I yearned for a larger audience and more steady work. Of course, I didn't know my life would suddenly require so much support, and I obviously had no idea we were about to become minor Internet celebrities. The irony was not lost on me. At the same time our business was becoming a pop-culture phenomenon and had a fraction of the world's attention, my family was growing. My heart was full and all I cared about was being close at home with my tribe.

Left: Chris and Isla
Below: Akil and Isla

It Was a Good Place to Work

by
Stephen Rusiniak

Like so many different aspects of our lives, too often we fail to consider what we have until it's gone, or the places we've been until we're no longer there. I recently revisited memories of my very first job. In retrospect, I can truly say that for the five years I was there, it was a good place to work.

The building where I was soon to be employed that summer before my high school senior year was still under construction and would become a nursing home when completed. It was a 20-minute walk from where I lived and less by bicycle—both important factors for a kid who'd recently earned his driver's license and longed to be behind the wheel of any type of vehicular transportation, but especially my dream vehicle: an older but very awesome Jeep-like pickup truck.

A job could go a long way in making truck ownership a reality, so I applied for employment in the kitchen at the nursing home. As I saw it, if I had to work anywhere, my employer might just as well feed me, too. And besides, the idea of working in a commercial kitchen sounded very cool to me. I was hired on the spot—just not for the kitchen job.

With the home's opening still two months away, there was little need for kitchen help just yet, but there were many other things for me to do instead. For the rest of the summer, I worked five days a week on various assignments throughout the building and grounds in preparation for September's grand opening. And early on, my initial paycheck—coupled with the thoughts of sitting behind the wheel of my dream truck—would provide all the motivation necessary for me happily to report for work each day. That is, until the morning when I discovered an even better reason to take that daily bicycle ride.

I'd been moving furniture into the empty rooms one morning when I looked out the window and noticed something odd in the parking lot below. Gone were all of the trucks and vans belonging to the contractors, and in their places were cars—lots of cars—filling almost every available parking space. Before I could consider what might be happening, I received a page over the PA system instructing me to report to the main office and to my boss. The parking lot mystery was about to be solved.

As I walked into the lobby just outside the main offices, I quickly learned two things: first, I'd discovered where all of the occupants from those parked cars had gone—the lobby was packed. And second, I noted that the vast majority of those crowding the lobby were female. Actually, there was one more thing that I was about to learn as well—something that should have been obvious—but just then I was totally oblivious to the obvious.

When I mentioned to my boss what I'd just witnessed, he simply smiled, but when I asked why so many people were all there, his smile immediately morphed into an are-you-really-that-stupid expression. Silly as this may sound, it hadn't occurred to me that the home still needed to be staffed.

My boss informed me that everyone in the lobby had responded to a newspaper ad and was applying for work. He also said, much to my absolute delight, that the vast majority of applicants applying would, in fact, be female. After all, females traditionally applied for the majority of available jobs such as nurses and nurses' aides, office help, housekeepers, kitchen staff and part-time weekend staff—which, by the way, I would eventually learn consisted primarily of high school and college-aged girls.

Of course, none of this had occurred to me when I'd first applied for work. But now, I had duly processed the information. Since learning that the ratio of female to male employees was about to put this 17-year-old boy squarely into a very happy minority, it would no longer be images of me sitting behind the wheel of some silly truck that would serve as the driving force bringing me to work each day. Yeah, I intended the driving pun.

This newfound information simply reaffirmed my original belief about being employed at this nursing home—it was a good place to work. And I'd soon be adding an obvious addendum—and it was a good place to meet girls. Before I'd leave the home's employment five years later, I would fall for three in particular.

We opened for business that September, and as foretold, the ratio of female to male employees that I'd heard about had come to pass. And for a guy whose previous dating experiences had been few and far between, my social life improved considerably. Almost immediately, I came to understand the meaning of the expression, "a beggar at a banquet," and to be honest, I was happy to be that beggar because no longer was I sitting home Saturday nights for the want of a date. And for a little while, I was perfectly content to sample the banquet's available offerings—unaware that someone was about to cause me to vacate my seat at this table.

I had seen her there before, and I liked what I saw—a pretty girl with blue eyes and long, wavy, dark hair. She had a Southern accent, but all I knew was that I loved the way everything that she said sounded, especially when she was saying it to me. And still, I kept my distance because even as both my social life and my confidence were growing, whenever I was near Caroline, my confidence levels would plummet. But as I kept my distance, I made it a point to be somewhere on the same floor where she happened to be assigned as an aid, hoping that she might notice me, hoping that maybe, somehow, we might exchange a few words, some small talk. But whenever I had the opportunity to do so, I didn't. That confidence thing was really starting to bother me.

One afternoon, I found myself alone with her in the pantry, about to serve dinner. I wanted to ask her out on a date, and I knew just what I'd say because I'd already said it to her a million times before, or at least in my dreams—but I just couldn't bring myself to say the words that I'd been planning to say.

And so the small talk between us continued for a while longer during which time I learned that she liked high school football games, drive-in movies, picnics, cherry soda, cinnamon gum, the scent of strawberries, and best of all, she liked me. We went out on a date, and then another, and another. One day it occurred to me: I had a girlfriend.

We dated for the last months of my senior year and all the next as I commuted to the local college, but after two proms, picnics in the park, kisses on a summer's day and all those nights when we just found it impossible to say goodbye, we did.

She left for college, started a new life and made new friends. And soon enough, I, too, would be making a new friend, and her name was Marcella.

She was working her usual assignment—escorting patients from their rooms to the dining room for dinner. And what I noticed was her smile, something she often did, something I found irresistible. That smile and her bubbly personality immediately put me on notice that there was something about this girl that I needed to learn more about, and to this end I set out to do just that.

It didn't take me long to learn everything that I needed to know about her. Besides the fact that I thought she was cute, she loved the outdoors—especially activities like hiking, skiing, bicycle rides and trips to the shore—just like I did. She was down to earth, honest and straightforward, and when she told me that she liked me, I wasn't surprised by her boldness. I drove her home that night by way of a local ice cream shop where we shared a sundae—our first date.

While it didn't happen overnight, it still happened. While I occasionally still went out on dates with other girls, Marcella went out with other guys—and this was fine with me, for a while. I was carrying a full course load at our local college and studying criminal justice while working almost full time to pay for school. And somewhere in this mix, as our relationship was becoming more and more serious, I began taking entrance exams to become a police officer.

The relevance of my relationship with Marcella and my attempts to land a career in law enforcement, for a while anyway, went hand in hand. We were both convinced that one day I'd have my career, and while I spent much of my time considering how to accomplish this, she was considering things, too—like marriage.

We'd been happy for some time, or so I thought. After a couple of years together, Marcella made no secret of the fact that she'd like us to marry. This wasn't really news to me, but with school and work and always another police exam somewhere on the horizon, I never thought all that much about marriage. Besides, my first concern was to get a job, specifically a job in law enforcement, a job that would provide my future family and me with the security of steady employment and a good income. Marcella wanted us to become engaged anyway. In fact, I refused to even consider such thoughts without first securing a good job—specifically some good cop job. She said that she understood, and I believed that she did too. We broke up not long afterward.

There's an old saying that goes, "When one door closes, another door opens." The astute reader may recall that I previously mentioned that while employed at the home, I'd fallen for *three* of my fellow employees—which, to be perfectly honest, may not be an entirely accurate statement. While I did, in fact, meet the third while still employed at the home, in truth, our relationship took off after I'd left. And if I were to write of my relationship with Karen, the verbiage necessary to approach the subject would surely require more allotted words than are afforded me now. In short, however, I can report that she became my partner, closest friend and eventually, she became the wife of a cop—oh yeah, I finally landed my dream job—from which, after a long and rewarding career, I recently retired. And as for Karen and me, she's still my wife and best friend, and after 37 years together, she remains the greatest part of my life.

Time and distance tend to cloud our dusty memory files, and as I happily approach my sixth decade, I can fondly look back and reaffirm the assessment once uttered by my younger self about that nursing home job I held so many years ago: "It was a good place to work." And you know what? It was.

Stephen and Karen, then and now

A Lunch to Remember

by
Clara Wersterfer

After marriage to an abusive man who was an alcoholic, I decided it would be best if I left my home state. I wanted to get as far away from my husband as I could so he wouldn't come looking for me. I'd been employed at a small stockbroker office, my first real job, and it broke my heart to leave the position I so loved and enjoyed.

I ended up in Richmond, Virginia, a place where friends lived. Within a week, I found an apartment and secured a job with a large stock brokerage firm. The work was clerical, but I was also a troubleshooter and someone to come to whenever a lot of digging or problem-solving was required.

Things went my way for the next few years. I kept to myself and did not even consider dating, even though some of the eligible guys in the office had asked. I was still licking my wounds and had not learned to trust any man.

One day, the office received a call from the Internal Revenue Service asking for a lot of information on a prominent client, so the call was forwarded to me. A young gentleman by the name of "James" spoke to me in the softest and kindest voice. I determined he was, indeed, with the IRS by looking up the phone number and calling his office. Once I was assured he was legitimate, I returned his call and we had a lengthy conversation about the information he needed.

Over the next two weeks, we talked on the phone every day and sometimes two or three times a day. Soon we were telling each other personal things. He found out I was divorced, and I learned he had not yet married. We were about the same age and liked many of the same foods and books. We seemed to have a lot in common.

On Thursday of the second week, he asked if I would go to lunch with him on Friday as he had to pick up the material in person. My heart skipped a few beats. At last we would meet, and if he looked as nice as he talked, it would be glorious. I was finally ready to move on, so I agreed. I went over all the required material, wrote the letter validating the package and took the paperwork to my boss for his approval and signature. Then I asked for, and received, an extra half-hour for lunch.

Friday morning, I got up earlier than usual in order to take extra time getting dressed and prettied up. Promptly at noon, a young man walked into the office carrying a bouquet of yellow roses. I knew it was the IRS agent even before Alice, the receptionist, came directly to me, rather than calling on the intercom, to announce I had a gentleman caller.

She leaned down and whispered, "Would you like me to go with you, so it doesn't look like you're a couple?"

Grinning, I shook my head no. Walking up to the counter, and wearing my best smile, I said, "I knew it was you the moment you spoke. No one else has such a pleasant voice." I shook his hand. He was beautifully dressed and quite nice looking. There was one surprise, however. He was black. I was in Virginia. It was the 1960s and segregation was still in the daily headlines.

My southern drawl may have fooled him into thinking I was black. I hadn't given color a thought. There seemed to be some sort of chemistry between us, even though we had never met.

When James asked where I would like to eat, I suggested a small diner down the street. The hour we spent eating and talking passed much too quickly. Several people looked at us oddly and whispered behind their menus, but we both ignored them and soon forgot they were there. I think we could easily have talked another hour. We both sighed when it was time to leave, sorry our time together was over.

He walked me back to my building, thanking me once more for my help and stumbling over what to say next. When we parted, I thanked him for the lunch, shook his hand again, holding it a little longer than the first time. I headed for the elevator without looking back.

Had we met 20 years later, there might have been a very different ending to this story.

A Job Like No Other

by
Patrick Hempfing

I had a successful 20-year professional career in banking, accounting and auditing. During those "bring home a check" days, I interacted with different types of people and experienced a little bit of everything. My relationships with coworkers were always the best part of my job, but I also had daily contact with customers.

As a bank branch manager, I made customers happy when I approved their loan requests. Conversely, others left my office disappointed and grumbling when I had to decline their applications. Who wouldn't enjoy playing with money for a living? I counted hundreds of thousands of dollars during my banking days. OK, the fact the money belonged to the bank and not me took away a bit of zest from the experience.

Later, I earned my college diploma as a nontraditional student. Not afraid of grueling experiences, obtaining a CPA license was next on my list. I can't say the four killer tax seasons were the highlight of my professional career. Get up and be on the job before sunrise. Work. Drink lots of coffee. Work. Drink lots of soda. Work. Go home in the dark. Kiss wife, sleep, and begin the process all over again. This described the first quarter of each year, a time when I romanced the coffee maker and soda machine more than my wife, Mattie. The dialogue with Mattie consisted more of moans and grunts than cohesive sentences. However, tax seasons always ended with a big party, and the rest of the year was more conducive to a happy marriage.

The moans and grunts continued after I switched careers again and became an internal auditor at a university. Usually, though, the noises came from the clients I audited. No one likes to see the auditor coming, so I didn't always feel the love. One client even nicknamed me "Columbo," as I always seemed to have another question.

Then, in 2004, Mattie gave birth to our beautiful daughter, Jessie. At age 44, I began yet another new job, this time as Mr. Mom. No, I didn't bring home a paycheck, but I didn't sit on the sofa and eat bonbons either. Nearly 10 years later, I can safely say being a stay-at-home dad has been the most demanding, and most rewarding, of my four jobs—without question.

Does it pay well? Not in dollars and cents, but in a lifetime of memories. How do the hours compare? Sixty to 80 hours per week during tax seasons were a piece of cake compared to the 24/7 rigors of Mr. Mom-hood. What noises do I hear? Oh, there have been plenty of comments of displeasure, and moans and grunts, as in my previous jobs. There has also been considerably more crying and a greater variety of fits, and I haven't even reached Jessie's teenage years. With that said, I wouldn't trade a single minute of my past 10 years watching my daughter grow from baby to toddler to almost a tween.

The job of Mr. Mom never gets boring, either. Each day, I wear numerous hats, some at the same time. Stay-at-home parenting requires not only the ability to multitask, but also the capacity to deal with ambiguous, rapidly changing conditions. I knock out some chores with no problem, while others require a bit more persistence. But I'm a patient guy by nature. However, although some tasks go as planned, other seemingly-simple undertakings quickly turn precarious and can be more difficult to predict than a customer's likelihood of defaulting on a loan.

When Jessie was three years old, she took Kindermusik classes at our church, and she always enjoyed them. I did, too, as Jessie was happy, learning and having fun. It didn't matter that I was the only man who was clapping, singing, jumping and holding hands with the rest of the Kindermusik moms and kids. I'm sure my tenor voice stood out on more than one occasion.

Jessie's Kindermusik class immediately preceded my evening tennis league. Being a good planner, I dressed in my tennis shorts, shirt and sneakers, packed my racket and water bottle and headed directly to the courts as soon as the class ended. Mattie met me at the courts and took Jessie home.

On this particular day, Jessie and I rode up the church

elevator with a little boy in the class and his mom. I wore a white T-shirt and gray tennis shorts. The string that supplemented the elastic waist on my shorts had come out in the laundry. I didn't see a need to throw away the shorts as they still fit nicely, so I continued wearing them, minus the string.

As the elevator started moving up, Jessie reached over to hold on to me. Unintentionally, she grabbed my shorts pockets from both sides and before I knew it, my stringless shorts were down below my knees. I yelled, "Jessie!" with only a jockstrap covering my assets. My T-shirt provided no help. Speechless and highly embarrassed, I quickly pulled up my shorts.

The mother in the elevator, who I'm sure saw my red face, along with a whole lot more of me, tried to put me at ease. She told me, "Oh, my son has pulled my blouse down on more than one occasion." As a "bean counter," I only had to worry about debits and credits, not exposing myself to the public. Let's face it—all jobs are like an elevator. They all have their ups and downs.

When Jessie began Pre-K, I decided to pursue a writing career while continuing to tackle the responsibilities of a stay-at-home parent. So far so good, except for the time I fell out of my desk chair and sprained my ankle . . . but that's another story.

I'll continue working hard to have a successful career while remaining a positive and often-present force in my daughter's life. I'm sure lots of exciting roles are in my future, like being a driver's education instructor and intimidating potential suitors. I plan to sign a few book deals, too. Of course, I'll be putting out the "fires" each day as a stay-at-home parent. Just the other night, I accidentally stepped on Jessie's doll and broke her leg. I superglued it back in place. I'm not making any guarantees on how long it will stay fastened, but I know when I handed Jessie her doll with two attached legs, her smile was worth a million dollars.

I love this job . . . especially when the sounds I hear are giggles, I'm fully clothed and each of Jessie's dolls has two legs.

Jessie and Patrick, on Father's Day 2009

Sure was Greek to Me!

by
Terri Elders

I'd heard that love might lurk no farther away than the next desk. Doubtful. Because of the kind of work I did, most likely Thomasinas or Harriets sat nearby, rather than Toms or Harrys. As for dicks, it had been so long since I'd dated anybody. I blushed whenever I recalled why men had them.

Sure, it was entirely my fault. I'd made poor choices. Why had I ever gone into social work? Why couldn't I have been a doctor, a lawyer or an engineer? Maybe because I'd no aptitude for or interest in those professions? Besides, I liked the kind of work I did. So maybe it was a fair trade . . . no love in my life, but a life that I loved.

I worked for a big state agency in a department devoted to maternal health. Aside from a lone pediatrician and one aging accountant, all the administrators and program supervisors in our basement headquarters were, like me, hopelessly female.

That pediatrician, though single, was half my age and already spoken for, and the elderly married accountant clung to his job solely to keep his equally aging bride in health insurance. Absolutely no prospects in sight.

If I'd been fresh out of grad school, it might have been different. I'd noticed young guys grouped together in the parking lot during our frequent fire drills. Though I congratulated myself for reaching my prime, in truth, my son was older than our pediatrician, and I'd been divorced for nearly 20 years. Additionally, I'd just returned from working overseas for a decade in developing countries where I'd rarely spy an eligible man in my age bracket.

Rarely? No. A more exact word would be "never." So my dating skills had oxidized . . . "rusty" was too generous a term. Even if an eligible man appeared on the scene, would I know how to react?

Then Jack, my noontime walking partner from upstairs in health statistics, came up with a plan. Daily we'd circle at a brisk pace around the hulking football stadium that occupied the park adjacent to our building. This day as we neared it, Jack edged close to me.

"Did I mention there's a new guy in my department? He's about your age. And he teaches Greek at night school."

I glanced sideways as we proceeded in our march. "My age? Teaches Greek? What's the catch? I bet he's married."

"Nope. Not anymore. Divorced for a few years."

I swallowed the bait. "So?"

"Well, Ginny and I thought you'd like to meet him. So we're planning to take him tomorrow for lunch at that new

Greek restaurant. Want to join us?"

"Oh, Jack," I gushed. "I love Greek myths. This will be great fun! And I'm a sucker for gyros."

"OK," Jack said as we headed back to the office, "And, by the way, his name is 'Dick.'"

I burst into laughter and disregarded the puzzled look on Jack's face.

It seemed strange to leave home the next morning without my usual apple slices and carrot sticks. A gyro would make a nice change.

Ginny and I were already ensconced in a booth when Jack and Dick arrived. The new statistician avoided making eye contact.

"How do you do?" I'd asked, plastering my face with a welcoming smile as Jack introduced us.

Dick nodded curtly, reaching for a menu. Strike one.

Ginny and Jack prattled on about the new health department pamphlet they were readying for the state Legislature. I fiddled with my gyros sandwich, poking the meat out and trying to slice it. Nearly too tough to chew, it was not nearly as tough as trying to make conversation with Dick.

"So," I'd offered for openers, "I understand you teach Greek."

He'd nodded, not glancing in my direction.

"Which of the tragedians is your favorite? I took a course in the history of the drama once, and realized I loved Sophocles the most."

"Don't read plays," Dick said, spooning up some of the mushroom soup he'd ordered. Turned out he couldn't eat anything spicy. Allergies, he claimed. Strike two.

"Have you ever been to Greece?" I continued, not one to give up easily. "I understand that the wine they call 'retsina' is delightful, and I've never found it at a Greek restaurant here in the States."

"Don't travel. Don't drink." Strike three. I shrugged.

"Dick likes classical music," Jack announced. "I told him you go to the symphony quite a bit." He winked at me from across the table. I could recognize a double-dog-dare-you when somebody tossed one my way.

I perked up. Maybe I hadn't struck out after all.

"Really? Wow. I have a couple of tickets for this Saturday afternoon for the performance at the music hall. I heard they might be doing some Vangelis. Would you like to be my guest?"

Dick slurped up the last of his soup, blotted his mouth and nodded.

Hey, I had a date!

That Saturday I dolled up, donning a summery dress and even a pair of heels. Dick picked me up in his pickup truck and drove silently to the theater. I struggled to keep up with him as we crossed the parking lot.

"Can't walk as fast as usual in these shoes," I pleaded, so he finally slowed down.

The good thing about a concert is that you've got a program to peruse during intervals, so conversational silences aren't quite so harrowing. I figure we poured over our respective programs so thoroughly we'd be able to pass a pop quiz, should the conductor announce one. We sat quietly through

Beethoven, Brahms and Bach. I peeked at Dick from time to time, but never caught him peeking at me.

For the finale, the orchestra played a medley from the scores of Vangelis films, culminating in the *Titles* tune from *Chariots of Fire*.

This is stirring music, folks, stunning. Raw, triumphant. It could melt the hardest heart. It could also make a fool of the most prudent woman. It made a fool of me.

I reached over and patted Dick's hand. And waited. And waited. He didn't grasp my hand in his. He didn't flinch or draw away. He didn't respond. At all.

After a minute or two, I slowly withdrew my hand.

When the concert ended, we hurried to his truck and drove back to my house.

Since we'd exchanged fewer than a hundred words all afternoon, I reluctantly asked if he'd like to come in for coffee. Surprisingly, he agreed.

Seated on my love seat, Dick began to talk. About his ex-wife, how he'd failed her, how he'd slipped into alcoholism then gradually got into recovery, how he had lost job after job, how grateful he was for his current employment and how much he loved teaching Greek.

The passion of Vangelis' music paled in comparison as Dick raved about the history of the language, Linear B and Linear A, indicatives, subjunctives, imperatives and optatives. He riffed for a while on declensions then segued into how his wife had never understood his passion for Greek.

"She studied Latin," he sneered, shuddering, nearly spilling coffee from his mug. His eyes lit up with spite. "Imagine!

She used to spend hours poring over Virgil's *Aeneid*. Did you ever hear of anything so foolish?"

Since this was the first question he'd asked me all day, I gave it grave consideration.

"I read a translation once in a history of literature course," I began.

Then I got playful. Dare I say it? I did. "I always liked how Dido listened patiently while Aeneas went on and on and on about his long and painful journey before he got to Carthage where he met her."

I shouldn't have worried. Dick didn't get my hint. He thanked me for the concert and the coffee, and then left.

Not long after, I ran into Ginny in the elevator at work.

"Did Jack tell you about Dick and my mom?"

"No," I answered, puzzled.

"I fixed them up to be partners for a square dance course she wanted to take. I think they're falling in love."

"Great."

Just a few days before, the Thomasina, who had the cube next to mine, had asked me how the online dating service I had enrolled in worked.

I demonstrated it, clicking on a message that had been sitting in my inbox for ages, unanswered because the gentleman lived half a continent away.

Ken's blurb said he'd traveled, lived overseas, liked dogs and books. I did, too, so I tapped out an answer to his message. Soon we graduated from email to phone calls.

During our first exchange, I asked if he ever studied languages.

"Tried to learn German once, but flunked out."

Did he like music?

"Brubeck, and Blood, Sweat and Tears."

Did he like to talk about his ex-wife?

"Never, ever. Wouldn't waste my breath."

When I told him about my fantasy of having an office romance with the statistician, he laughed.

"Don't worry, baby. You didn't miss anything. Retsina's not all that hot. Had some once in Mallorca. Tastes like turpentine."

It was my turn to laugh. Love indeed had been lurking at the next desk in the form of Thomasina, who showed me where Ken had been hiding . . . in my Social.net inbox.

When Ken and I were married eight months later, I'd remembered why men had what they had. Just like a myth come true.

Incompetency Takes the Cake

by
Marcia Gaye

Dee, our new department manager, was young, bubbly, friendly and totally inept at her job. This last trait didn't bother me much since my interaction with her was minimal. As the lone clerical-data person, I flew mostly under the radar. As long as I shuffled my papers in the right order and filed them in the proper folders, I was free to roam about our cubicles, laughing at Dee's jokes and enjoying her home-baked treats. Home-baked "bribes" would be a more accurate description.

Dee passed around cookies and generous slices of cakes. She did take the title of manager seriously, though. She seriously managed to avoid her duties, convincing the other office staff to do them for her by offering sweetly frosted incentives. It worked OK for a couple of weeks.

It so happened that one of our number had decided to

actually stick to the perpetual diet we all claimed to be on. Kind-hearted actuary Marilyn never shirked her duties and was known throughout the entire company as capable and trustworthy. She had been doing her job at the same desk for years, never making waves and always with a smile. But Marilyn's sweet disposition took a sour turn after she had forced herself to decline treat after treat while absorbing the extra work piled on by Dee's inactivity.

One afternoon, the proffer of a chunk of delicious cinnamon cake was met with a snappish refusal. "No thank you, Dee. Why don't you just do some work instead of wasting time? You aren't here to act as our private pastry chef!"

Dee's face fell like a punctured soufflé. She exited the room and in a few minutes, Marilyn was summoned to the CFO's office.

Fortunately, our actuary's well-honed reputation stood strong. Because the officer had never heard Marilyn speak ill of anyone, he took her cue and scrutinized Dee's performance. Finding it lacking, he made an inquiry to human resources. When asked how they had hired such an incompetent person, they denied having played a part in it. They said she was hired on the basis of the interview conducted by the director of finance. The director admitted that he had interviewed Dee but had made no such recommendation. He thought the CFO had approved the hire. Yes, Dee had filed an application. Yes, she had been interviewed. Yes, she had shown up at the reception desk late the next day balancing a fresh cinnamon cake and a box of personal desk paraphernalia. When asked for her credentials by the receptionist, she replied, "I'm Dee, the new department manager, reporting for my first day. Here, have a piece of celebration cake."

She then had simply waltzed into the office, introduced herself by way of cake, and set up her desk. Within hours, she had her badge and keys and had filed the requisite official paperwork.

We were never quite sure if Dee had been so naïve as to interpret the musings of her interviewer as a hard offer for the position, which is what she claimed, or if she had been inspired by George Costanza's antics on TV's *Seinfeld* and strong-armed her way into a paying job via blatant deception. To tell you the truth, it didn't matter to me. I came away with the best recipe ever. Even though I altered it a tad to make it my own, I still call it Dee's Cinnamon Cake, and when it wins blue ribbons, my victory is sweet.

Cinnamon cake

Left on the Doorstep

by
Mona Dawson

I took a summer job in an electronics factory where my mom worked. At the time, Mom delivered the mail plus made coffee in each division of the plant. It was a big job, and since she was so outgoing and friendly, she knew everyone. And everyone knew her.

After a few days of training, I saw a guy I went to high school with at one of the coffee stations. We weren't friends in school because we moved in different crowds; he was a "greaser," and I was a "frat." But I liked the way he looked, so grown up after a few years out of school. We flirted a bit. He'd comment on my short skirt and long legs, I'd comment on his perfectly groomed beard in the age of shabbiness.

Mom noticed us talking a few times over coffee but kept to herself. That is until she caught him staring at me one afternoon when I passed him in the hallway.

"Hey! Look out, Dan. That's my daughter you're staring at!" she warned him.

"Your daughter? But she's so tall and you're so short," Dan responded.

"Well, she takes after her father, so watch yourself." Mom turned back to her coffee-making duties, trying to conceal her smile. She liked Dan a lot—he wasn't the long-haired type I sometimes brought home.

Working in the same company as my mom had its moments. She watched me from afar. Everyone at work knew I was her daughter and that I was off limits to them, a difficult situation for me.

Then one evening, I found myself at home pacing back and forth, because that's what I do when I'm nervous. But I had never felt nervous quite like this before. This was a new feeling for me. I was expecting my older brother's friend, Doug, to come to the back door for our date. I'd known him for a long time. I never looked at him as a boyfriend, only as a friend. I did like him, just not in a romantic way. He'd asked me earlier if I wanted to go to a party in Berkeley with him and I'd said I would. But it wasn't Doug who made me so nervous.

I was also expecting a knock at the front door. I'd accepted a date from Dan after I'd already said yes to Doug. With any luck, Doug would come first, and I'd tell him I wasn't going out with him. What a mess I'd gotten myself into. I thought for sure I would throw up. My parents were out for the evening, so I had no backup. They were usually my support when I got myself into situations like this.

Dan had called me about an hour earlier, and my heart had stopped. I couldn't believe he'd called. Besides the casual flirting, I didn't think he had any interest in me since he was so popular with all the other single girls at work.

"What are you doing tonight?" he asked after my hello.

"Nothing," I lied.

"OK. Well, since I'm doing nothing and you're doing nothing, why don't we do nothing together?" Clever and original, don't you think?

"OK," I said as I checked my appearance—my long hair, my top and my jeans. *Am I fat?* I thought. *Or am I too tall for him? Why did he call me? Couldn't he get a date with anyone else? Why did I agree?*

Just as he knocked on the front door, I heard a knock at the back door. I froze. *OK, let's think this out. I'll let Dan in first, and then I'll excuse myself and go to the back door.* I ran to the front door, but Doug's knocking on the back door kept getting louder.

As I opened the front door, Dan asked if I was ready to go. He was my height, with a neatly trimmed beard, short hair, a nice shirt, tan cord Levi's and blue-blue eyes. He was just too cute.

I tried to keep my heart from plugging my throat and choking me. I took a deep breath. "Sure, come on in. But can you just wait a second?" I ran to the back door.

"Hey kid, let's move," Doug said, smiling. He was heavyset with curly dark hair, and he was not very well dressed. In fact, he was grungy. But he was a sweet guy and one of the most fun of all my brother's friends. I felt safe with him.

"Uh, yeah. Why don't you come in for a second?" I needed to throw up.

Confused, Doug entered the house, and we walked into the living room where Dan stood waiting. They had been in the same class in school a few years earlier, so I re-introduced them to each other. They visited for a few minutes, Dan saying he just got out of the Army, Doug saying his draft classification was 4-F. Then Doug looked over at me and nodded, as he understood what was happening.

"I gotta get going, I'm off to Berkeley," he said, smiling at me.

"Thanks for stopping by," I said, grinning with relief. Doug left out the back door as Dan and I headed out of the front door.

"What did he want?" Dan asked.

"I said I'd go to Berkeley with him." I was prepared for him to kick me out of the car.

"Oh," was his only reply.

Dan drove a black MGB GT convertible. It was such a cool car, and I hoped he'd drive it fast. He didn't. Still, the evening turned out to be the best date I'd ever been on. We went to a local diner where all the kids hung out. We cruised around in his cool car. We talked about everything and laughed nonstop at nothing. Late in the evening, we ended up at his studio apartment. A low counter separated the bed from the kitchen. There was little room to move around, a true bachelor's pad.

Having been out of the Army for a short while, Dan had missed the current music the rest of us listened to. I loved the Beatles, Bob Dylan, Joan Baez, Donovan and the Rolling Stones. Dan had only Righteous Brothers and Beach Boys albums. He put on some music. I noticed his dated collection and teased him.

We made fun of each other's music—his was square and mine was hippie. He tried to be serious, but I laughed so hard I couldn't breathe. I couldn't calm down. He wanted to kiss; I couldn't hold back my laughter as he tried desperately to make his move. He wanted soft, quiet music and tried to get cozy; I had trouble being serious. Instead, we sat on the floor, at the end of the bed, and talked for what seemed like hours.

When it was time for him to take me home, we drove in silence. He walked me to my door. After standing on the porch a minute or so, he kissed me goodnight and said, "I had the best time of my life tonight. I never laughed so hard. You are so funny. But, I'd never marry a girl like you."

Shocked, I snapped back, "So who asked you to?" and I slammed the door in his face.

I remind him of this on each anniversary. We just celebrated our 44th.

Their wedding day, 1970

Mona and Dan when they were dating

CHAPTER FOUR

Open
Mouth . . .

. . . insert foot!

Read the Label

by
Belinda Cohen

Fresh out of nursing school, I worked as a substitute for various doctors in the region. One day, I'd be changing catheters in the geriatric ward of the hospital. The next day, I'd be in the gynecologist's office warming tubes of K-Y Jelly. Never a dull moment.

After a year of making the rounds, I thought I'd seen it all. I was, after all, a professional. So when I got a call from a local urologist's office, I was happy to oblige.

The third patient of the day was 38-year-old Tom. He was a good-looking man with a military buzz cut and broad shoulders. His wife had recently delivered their third child, and Tom explained, "If my wife gets pregnant again, I'm gonna shoot myself."

Clearly, it was time for a vasectomy.

I began with the usual questions. "Are you taking any

medications?" He went down a list of pills he'd pop for post-workout pain.

"You'll need to stop taking ibuprofen and aspirin. If you feel sore after exercise, just take Tylenol." After a few more questions, Tom was ready for the doctor.

"We need to complete a simple genital examination," Dr. Amor said, washing his hands and slipping on the plastic gloves that make a man instinctively flinch.

We eased Tom's feet into the stirrups. I stood next to the doctor who sat on a round stool, placing him at eye-level with the man's groin.

"Belinda, can you spray the antiseptic on his skin? It's in the yellow bottle over there." I looked on the counter, retrieved the yellow bottle and soaked Tom's jewels with the cleanser.

Dr. Amor continued explaining. "We'll be looking for varicose veins, epididymal cysts and any unusual testicular sensitivity."

Tom laid back with his eyes closed and his feet in the stirrups, his legs spread wide apart. He swallowed several times and took short, panting breaths. I stayed still, knowing that a young woman watching this exam is about as pleasant for the man being examined as taking a baseball to the groin.

Dr. Amor rolled Tom's balls between his thumb and forefinger. He scrunched his face and stared, confused for a moment.

"Is there something you need, doctor?" I asked in my nurse voice.

He darted his eyes to Tom's guy parts. He took three

short tugs trying to free his hands. They didn't budge.

It took me a moment to register that Dr. Amor's hands were glued to Tom's nuts. I covered my mouth in shock and my gaze shot toward the counter.

The yellow container was clearly labeled, "Adhesive." The orange one said, "Antiseptic."

Shit.

The doctor carefully slid his hands out of the gloves and informed Tom we needed to step out of the room. "Just relax a moment," he said to the man in the stirrups with deflated gloves gently swaying from his testicles.

Safely out of hearing range, we let our laughter roar. "How do you unglue plastic from a guy's balls?" I asked.

Dr. Amor rubbed his chin. "We can't send him home like that." His response sent me into a second round of giggle fits.

"What about bandage scissors? We can put the knob against his skin and trim the glove. He can wash off any residual plastic in the shower at home."

He nodded, and we returned to the exam room with straight faces.

Tom never did come back for that vasectomy. I just hope he didn't decide that shooting himself was better than a second trip to the urologist's office.

Weather Girl Goes Rogue

by
Faune Riggin

I'm a professional. How do I know? Because I have a professional profile on LinkedIn, of course! Sometimes when I look back at my early career, I wonder how I ever got to where I am today. I've been with KZIM-KSIM radio in the St. Louis area since 2001, where I produce and host the *Morning News Watch*. I've also worked in music radio. I've been presented more awards than I can count, including awards for broadcasting excellence. I was even named one of the top 10 best radio programmers in the nation for small market radio by *Radio Ink* magazine. But everyone who has worked with me in radio, and the organizations who bestowed me those awards, must not have heard how I got my start, as the chief weather forecaster for the CBS television affiliate in western North Dakota.

As a kid, I had always admired the people on TV. I never

thought I could be one of them. So when I was hired at the North Dakota station, I was over the moon. My wish of being on TV had come true—I had landed the job of weather person.

My forecasts were done in front of a chroma-key green-screen—the weather maps showed up behind me. What many people might not know is when they see a weather map behind the weather person, the weather map shows up facing the opposite way on the in-studio monitor. For the person doing the reporting, everything is backward. Even though I had practiced, I sometimes had a hard time navigating the green-screen. But I was determined.

During my very first weather telecast—which I was so excited about—I saw the maps and accidentally pointed at Washington State while talking about the New England states. Then I saw myself backward in the monitor and became confused. I looked at the news anchors and asked them, "Who took New England?" After they laughed at my on-air joke, I fell into a groove and my broadcast flowed with ease. But remember, it was LIVE television and anything could happen.

Part of my broadcast was to report on a cluster of thunderstorms in the upper Midwest. I pointed out the system on the lee side of the Rocky Mountains then said, with complete confidence, "Storms are *pussing acrotch* Minnesota."

Yes, "pussing acrotch," not "pushing across."

I was mortified. I felt my TV career was over. I looked dead into the camera and said, "Ladies and gentlemen, from now on, all storms will be moving 'toward' locations." The station received an outpouring of both laughter and complaints after that. My error even gained me a giant role on the station's Christmas blooper tape.

Not to be outdone during that same news broadcast, one of the anchors—who was female—spoke about the U.S. Postal Service collecting grocery donations. Area residents were asked to put non-perishable foods, like canned goods or boxed meals, in bags provided for collection by letter carriers. The groceries were then distributed to local food banks. With the best of intentions—and following my clustered-weather segment—she said, "Well, we know your mailman is hoping his bags are a lot heavier today." Roaring laughter erupted from the co-anchor, sports guy, camera operators and yours truly. Yes, folks—live television can become its own monster.

I am happy to report that radio is my niche. I loved TV, but with radio, I can get away with wearing pajamas to work, and I don't have to deal with the green-screen!

Faune at work at KZIM/KSIM

Check, Please

by
Renee Hughes

At one point in my career back in the 1980s, I worked for an accounting department for several weeks to help process payments. If an incoming payment didn't include the customer's account number, which was required so our office would know where to apply the money, it was plopped onto the pile on my desk. Being an auditor by both nature and career choice, I relished digging through files to match the payments to the proper accounts. Sick, sick puppy, I know, but it was the perfect job for me.

A couple of traveling auditors from out of town sometimes helped me, but they were usually busy with other duties. I was lucky that I didn't have to travel. The company ran two shifts, and the traveling auditors had to work seven days a week, 12 hours a day. In fact, two of them took turns doing the same job, one on day shift and the other on night shift. They shared a hotel room, swapped work shifts and even shared one bed while I got to go home to my own bed every night.

After a few weeks on this project, I became proficient at check sleuthing. One check stumped me, however. There was no account number on the check, so I couldn't figure out where to apply the payment. There was a handwritten number at the bottom of the check, but it didn't relate to any account number in our system.

I thought the handwritten figures might be a telephone number, but when I tried calling, there was no answer. As luck would have it, there was also a phone number pre-printed on the check, so I dialed it. A friendly lady answered, and I explained I had received a payment without an account number. "Is the gentleman who signed the check paying bills for someone else, maybe his mom or a teenager who is away at college? Perhaps for a grandparent?" I asked. "There is a handwritten number of some kind on the bottom of the check, and it might be a phone number, but when I called it, there was no answer."

"Could you give me the handwritten number?" she asked. "Maybe I'll recognize it."

Giving her the number, she explained to me that her husband handled all the bills and the checkbook, and he would be home around 7 P.M. "I'll ask him about the check and one of us will call back to let you know."

Before I hung up, I thanked her then gave her my work number, saying she could leave a message with the person working the next shift, since I would be off work at 7 P.M.

When I reported to the office the next morning, imagine my shock when the night-shift personnel informed me they had received a call the previous evening from an irate man who inquired as to who in the world was the imbecile who gave his girlfriend's phone number to his wife.

Oops! But honestly, who was the real imbecile?

Renee hard at work

Learning to Keep My Mouth Shut

by
Petey Fleischmann

My husband, Bob, has a tremendous sense of humor. I do, too. But my problem, so I'm told, is that I don't know when to keep my mouth shut. Bob often tells me I need to think before I speak. I argue the point, but perhaps it's true.

In 1974, I was selected for a position with a federal government utility. Within three years, I was selected as the secretary to the head of human resources (HR), working for an incredible man whom we'll call Harry.

During my time in HR, the agency conducted various exercises on how to save money. Most of these budget exercises boiled down to personnel costs and how the agency could cut costs without conducting a reduction-in-force (RIF). Harry and many of his HR supervisors were heavily involved in these budgeting issues.

In addition to, and because of, these extra cost-reduction exercises, my normally heavy workload increased with the added workload from our parent agency in Washington, D.C. But I got the work done and I did it well.

After a particularly difficult few months of nonstop deadlines and demands, I began to wish I had roller skates just to get from office to office. I even quit taking the elevator because it was too slow. One day, Harry called and asked me to bring my steno pad and to come up to the administrator's office—the top position in this agency—to take notes for the next go-round of budget cuts. "Of course," I said, "I'll be right up." *Would some of my friends lose their jobs?* I wondered. *Would I?!*

I sat for a moment, calmed my trembling knees, wiped my sweaty palms on my pants and tried to steady my voice before I left my desk. *The administrator is just another person*, I thought. *He is NOT God. He is NOT God*, I repeated in my head.

When I arrived, the administrator invited me into his office and shut the door. I felt like a coffin lid had closed. I observed a half dozen HR supervisors sitting at the meeting table, all looking as if their best friend had just died. Harry wouldn't make eye contact with me. My knees began to tremble again, and my mouth felt like I'd just eaten a plate full of cotton, seeds and all. I was sure this meant the end of my job, just one more budget cut. As I sat down, I noticed my steno pad was damp where I had been clutching it.

The administrator pulled up another chair, sat down and began to tell me how serious the budget issues were. He explained that HR was over budget and that he had no choice but to cut one position in HR. "I'm sorry," he said, lowering his eyes to the table. Then there was a very brief moment of silence as people waited for me to absorb that I was the one to go.

Missing my mouth filter, but not missing a beat, I turned to my wonderful boss and said, "Harry, I'm sorry to see you go. I'm really going to miss you."

The laughter that followed was deafening, and the two people who laughed the loudest were the administrator and Harry. I sat in disbelief, wondering why, once again, I had been unable to keep my mouth shut.

After the laughter had died down, I found out no one was on the chopping block. They were playing a joke on me. Instead, the administrator presented me with a nice award. My hand was still damp and trembling as I shook his and accepted the honor.

It turned out to be the best meeting ever, and I didn't even have to take notes.

Petey volunteering for more work!

What Denomination?

by
Karen Gaebelein

My first real job was in customer service at a local bank. I had no customer service background and knew very little about banking. Did I mention that I was shy and disliked math, as well? So, there I was—quiet, inexperienced and with a wardrobe that looked like it had jumped off the pages of a girls' parochial-school catalog—ready to conquer the world of the banking biz.

During the training period, my head spun with all the information I tried to absorb. I knew that my brain was going to explode with debits, credits, balancing, products, customer service—and all with a big smile. Stock on pain relievers must have skyrocketed in value during this period. I left each workday with a throbbing brain and a sore face from grinning at customers for hours on end.

The sofa in the lunchroom called to me every time I

took my break. It looked so inviting. I knew if I laid on it, all that information dancing in my head would ooze out of my ears and fall onto the floor. I sat upright to avoid that happening and to remain determined and focused.

I quickly learned that some of the banking services were seasonal. We sold more money orders at the beginning of each month. Christmas Club money was released in time for everyone to get their shop on by Thanksgiving and traveler's check sales increased during peak vacation time.

It was great fun to hear about our customers' vacation plans when they came in for their traveler's checks. I enjoyed hearing about all the great sights they planned to see and places they would visit. It became routine for travelers to come back and regale us with wonderful stories of their trips. Another advantage was seeing awesome photos of their adventures.

One particular traveler's check purchase remains etched in my memory. The client, a lovely woman who had saved her money to make a trip out West, was so excited she could barely contain herself.

I can still picture her face, so alive and happy, as she told me of her plans to visit San Francisco, Arizona and Las Vegas.

In the midst of her excitement, she advised how much money she had for her transaction. I excused myself for a moment to get the traveler's checks.

When I returned with the tray of checks, I began to complete the paperwork. I started by asking her, "What denomination?"

She flashed a big smile and proudly replied, "Baptist."

I told her I would be right back and immediately went into one of the senior staff offices, out of earshot of my excited customer. I closed the door, giggled and explained to my colleague what had happened.

She smiled and said, "You have to collect yourself and get back out there and finish the transaction." I knew she was right, so I took a deep breath and went back to my seat.

I turned the tray, waved my hand over the denominations and tried again. "OK, what would you like, a combination of 10s, 20s and 50s?"

She laughed and said, "Oh, that's what you meant. Silly me."

We completed her transaction, and that client remained one of my favorite customers for many years. She sent us postcards then came in and showed us photos of her trip when she returned.

Since that time, whenever I hear the word "denomination," I cannot help but chuckle as I remember that bright smile and her proud statement, "Baptist."

A Slip of the Tongue

by
Camille DeFer Thompson

I thought I'd won the golden ticket to Willy Wonka's Chocolate Factory. Thirty-something and single, just hired by the sheriff's office, I envisioned uniformed men stumbling over themselves, catering to my every whim. Little did I know the experience would turn out to be more like a mine-field than a candy store.

Selected for my expertise in information technology, a unique skill in the late 1980s, I found myself answering the call of frustrated tech-challenged co-workers on a daily basis. One morning, I spotted a gaggle of testosterone-loaded colleagues hunched over the monitor of the deputy in the cubicle across the aisle from mine. Before long, my curiosity got the best of me. "You need some help over there?"

"Danno can't get out of Excel," came the baritone reply from an onlooker.

This won't take long, I thought. *I'll dazzle them with some fancy diagnostic somersaults then graciously accept their offers to fetch a fresh cup of coffee for my trouble.*

I sauntered over and paused to let the contingent of spectators make way for the pro, feeling their eyes bore into my lithe form. I leaned over a bit to accentuate my allure and surveyed the paralyzed PC. I tapped a couple of keys. Nothing.

"Hmmm . . . " I said, scratching my head with a sexy French-manicured nail. "Looks like you're hung, Danno," I said, contemplating my next expert analytical maneuver.

Tap, tap, tappity-tap. Nada. "Geez, you're really hung."

Tappity, tappity-tap. Zip. "Yep," I said, engrossed in the task, ignoring their muffled snorting. "You're seriously hung."

An explosion of laughter shook me out of my system-support stupor.

My face on fire, I hit Ctrl-Alt-Delete and slunk off to the ladies' room to formulate a keystroke combination to reboot the last 15 minutes of my life.

As network administrator for the new county jail under construction, I soon learned that the majority of the sworn staff assigned to the massive high-security campus was unfamiliar with the mystifying world of user ID's, diskettes and email. This afforded the strapping young bucks any number of opportunities to come sniffing around my office. One burly, barrel-chested lieutenant was a regular visitor, offering a variety of lame excuses to shoulder his way in. He made himself comfortable in the chair next to my desk and regaled me with tales of his tough-guy persona.

One morning, Lt. Bragsalot stopped by just as I was about to enjoy a morning pick-me-up. He crowed about his latest show of unparalleled courage during a recent encounter with an unruly inmate. "I slapped the cuffs on that thug, looked him straight in the eye and told him . . . uh . . . I told him . . . "

"What?" I asked, looking up when he stopped mid-sentence. "Told him *what?*"

His face lit up like the flashing beacon atop a patrol car. "You're not . . . uh . . . going to eat that now . . . are you?"

I reached behind him and tossed the flaccid yellow peel into the trashcan. "Yeah, why not?" I replied, still oblivious to his rising discomfort.

"Uh . . . well . . . I mean . . . "

Just as I bit the top off my suggestive snack, he stammered, "I gotta go." He fled the scene like a thief with a bulging bag of booty.

Who knew a common tropical delight could disarm a Sonny-Crockett wannabe in one mouthful?

My duties with the department included a turn as IT manager for the automated 911 dispatch system at the Emergency Operations Center (EOC). Housed in a 1950s-era underground bunker, built to serve as a bomb shelter during the Cold War, the windowless, dingy white concrete walls proved to be a depressing work environment. To lighten the atmosphere, the EOC manager encouraged camaraderie among the small assortment of sworn and civilian staff. A striking figure in his starched uniform, Captain Chiseled maintained a dignified demeanor, but often joined in the water cooler conversations, careful to never breach the line between superior and pal.

Deb, a chain-smoking, take-no-prisoners divorced mother of two—think Carla of *Cheers* fame—was the civilian receptionist for non-emergency calls. Despite her edgy persona, she maintained a calm, authoritative tone over the phone.

One day, a handful of co-workers gathered in her cubicle. The topic turned to favorite foods. I commented that some years back I had acquired a taste for venison, one of my former mother-in-law's signature dishes.

"Oh, yeah," Deb said, in her distinctive raspy voice. "Preparing wild game is tricky. You gotta know how to cook out that gamey taste. I got to be pretty good in the kitchen growing up, helping my mother."

"I'll eat just about anything," the captain said, "except beef tongue. That's one dish I've never cared for."

Without missing a beat, the proud cook blurted, "Oh, Captain, I could slip you some tongue, and you'd never know it."

I watched Deb's face kaleidoscope through 50 shades of crimson. Just as the collective gasp died down, and the roar of belly laughs reached its crescendo, her phone rang.

We struggled to muffle our guffaws. Ever the consummate professional, my co-worker closed her eyes for a moment, stiffened her shoulders then picked up the receiver. "Sheriff's Office, may I help you?"

Captain Chiseled ushered us out of Deb's office, and then motioned for me to follow him.

Crap, what now? The only civilian witness to the incident, I wondered if I was in trouble for . . . what? Unauthorized amusement? I prepared myself for a tongue-lashing.

"Sit down," he said, gesturing to the sofa against the wall opposite his desk. He glanced around the room, avoided eye contact then settled into his high-backed executive chair. "You know Deb pretty well. This is awkward, but . . . has she ever talked about . . . me?

Oh. My. God. Did he think for even a nanosecond that Deb's slip of the tongue was intended as a come-on?

He adjusted some papers on his desk. "I don't want to embarrass her, but if she needs to be spoken to . . . "

I interrupted his rambling.

"Captain," I said. "I can assure you that Deb did not mean for her comment to be interpreted as anything other than cooking a slab of meat."

He leaned back, ran his fingers through his hair then let out a long breath. "Right. Thanks." He rose and opened his office door. "That'll be all."

The unfortunate tongue incident never crossed anyone's lips again. Peace was restored to the bomb shelter.

Camille still enjoys her morning snack.

Dorothea's Restaurant

by
Barbara Carpenter

Ranking in the top 10 percent of my high school senior class didn't mean much to me at the time. In the first place, college was not an option, for there was no way I could afford it. My class adviser tried valiantly to convince me to apply for scholarships. And, in the second place, I was already engaged to be married the following spring.

Shortly after graduation, my father moved the family back to the small town where I had attended the first six years of grade school. The boy I had dated for almost three years—yes, since I was 15—lived and worked a hundred miles away. He drove those miles north just to spend a few hours with me nearly every weekend. During the rest of the week, I was at loose ends and lonely, and I didn't know what to do.

I soon discovered that you really can't go home again. Friendships I had formed the first six years in the little town had all but disappeared in the intervening six years since my return. What to do? A neighbor told my mother that a local restaurant needed another waitress. I needed a job, so I applied.

On that beautiful September morning, I walked the eight blocks—not quite half the width of the town—to the small restaurant. A door in the center of the white-block building opened onto a cozy, warm interior, and wide windows on each side of the restaurant's door provided lots of light, enhanced further by smaller windows on the outer walls.

I approached the three-sided bar in the center of the room. A dark-haired girl, dressed in the requisite white waitress uniform, greeted me. I told her that I had come to apply for a job. She nodded, turned her back and disappeared through an opening in the back wall. My confidence disappeared with her.

A short, older woman, dishtowel draped across one shoulder, came slowly through that door. She did not smile. She wiped her hands across her apron, peered at me through rimless glasses and stopped directly in front of me, the bar between us.

"Yes?"

I swallowed. "Our neighbor told me that you might want to hire another waitress?" I hated the shaky question in my reply. The woman raised her head slightly and looked at me through the bottom of her bifocals. Her fair skin and faded red hair, now mostly gray, showed that she had once been a beauty.

"It's a split-shift. Hours from 10 to 2 and 4 to 8, five days a week. You'd take turns with my other girl on Saturdays, 10 to 2. Minimum wage, plus tips. What's your name?"

"Barbara," I said. "Barbara Elliott. We live in John Little's house on North Walnut, across Route 45. We lived here before, just a couple blocks south, on Pine Street. Beside the park." I could hear myself babbling.

"I'll let you know tomorrow," the woman said. She did not smile. I thanked her and left, thinking that if she was the owner, she must be a bear of an employer.

The next afternoon, Dorothea Mullikin—the lady from the restaurant, who I quickly learned was indeed the owner and boss—came to our home. My mother answered the door, and I heard a gravelly voice say, "I've come to tell your girl that she can start work tomorrow."

And that's how I became the split-shift waitress at Dorothea's Restaurant, the gathering place for local businessmen and farmers, every morning, noon and many evenings. It didn't take long to learn the routine. Dorothea didn't require Shirley, the other waitress, or me to wear uniforms, which was a plus. Shirley just chose to wear them.

Neither did it take long for the loquacious farmers and locals to discover that I was an innocent, inexperienced babe-in-the-woods to their practical jokes and banter. One particularly busy noon hour, both Shirley and I kept Dorothea busy in the kitchen.

"Order!" She called, filling them almost as quickly as we delivered them to her. I had learned how to carry three plate lunches at once, balancing one on my left forearm as I carried one in each hand. I entered the bar with three orders, smiling at each man as I placed his lunch before him.

In the center of the three-sided bar was a narrow island with long, tall, two-sided shelves laden with candy bars, cigarettes and sundries. I felt someone move behind me and turned to see Jack, our landlord, reaching for a pack of cigarettes. I glanced at him and smiled in recognition.

"I'm sorry," he said. "I didn't want to bother you. I'll just add this to my bill." He held up the pack of cigarettes and moved to the other side of the counter.

"Jack, you old dog. You left your dirty handprint on her rear!" One of the old guys roared with laughter.

When I turned around to look, the whole counter full of them exploded into loud guffaws.

"Look at Jack's face," he continued. "You old goat! Your face is red as a beet!" So was mine, and from then on, I often became the butt of their jokes . . . pun intended.

Such was my life in the restaurant. I learned to deal with it, keeping a smile on my face, and even came to enjoy the banter. Rarely did anyone cross the invisible line that would get him thrown out of Dorothea's Restaurant.

Her specialty was pie, any kind of pie. She made pineapple cream, raisin, chocolate, lemon, apple, coconut cream, even rhubarb and gooseberry, but the absolute best was cherry. One weekday, after most of the lunch crowd had come and gone, Dr. Black, the resident chiropractor and genuinely nice man, came in for a late lunch.

I delivered Dr. Black's order, and then busied myself washing down tables and straightening up. Only a few diners remained. The day's pies, placed on that center island, beckoned to Dr. Black, who kept himself in top physical condition. Only his white hair indicated that he might have left his youth behind.

"Boy, that cherry pie looks good," he told Dorothea, who had come out to chat with him.

"It's worth every penny," she said and chuckled. "I think you can afford it."

"Oh, I don't know," he answered. He patted his lean abdomen.

"Come on," Dorothea continued. "You only live once." Finished with my task, I joined her in the center.

"It really is good, Dr. Black," I said. "Would you like a little piece?"

For the space of perhaps three seconds, there was no sound in the restaurant. Then Dorothea snorted . . . actually snorted! Dr. Black choked on his coffee. They exchanged glances, and my boss began to laugh. Poor Dr. Black tried his best not to, but he chuckled.

"What?" Bewildered, I looked at both of them. "What did I say?"

Dorothea turned toward me, shook her head, glanced back at her customer and tried to sober up, at least a little. "Why don't you gather up the menus and cross off what we're out of for this evening," she suggested, that devilish grin still trembling on her lips.

Later that evening, as she and I prepared the restaurant for the following morning's crowd, she asked me to sit down for a minute. Then, explicitly, she explained to me the unspoken context of my faux pas.

"And that is why, my dear, you should never, never ask a man if he 'wants a little piece,' unless you are prepared to give him one." It was a lesson I never forgot.

Barbara at age 18 (1959)

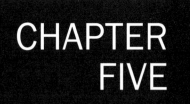

CHAPTER FIVE

I Am Woman

Watch me soar!

Following in Daddy's Footsteps

by
Janet Sheppard Kelleher

I missed my daddy. Two years after his death, the accountant I worked for retired, so I mulled over the classified ads looking for a change. *Aha! I'll drive an ice cream truck!* I said to myself when I read the employment ad.

At the interview, the boss, loving my enthusiasm, hired me on the spot and gave me a cute red Chevy ice-cream truck. Set to make millions, I knew this would be the best job ever—outside all day, no real responsibility, just driving and selling Nutty Buddies to gap-toothed little kids. The only drawback was listening to the truck's song "Jack and Jill went up the hill . . . " for hours on end.

Alas, I soon discovered that people with freezers and air-conditioned houses weren't much interested in buying Popsicles on the street from a tie-dyed college kid in blue jeans. Close to broke, I made an executive decision. The idea was so brilliant that I should have changed my major from math to marketing.

Crumpling up the "safe-neighborhood" maps my boss had given me, I turned up the music volume and drove my Daddy's old insurance route, which lived in my head.

A captivating black lady dozed in a rocking chair on her porch, but not for long with 120 decibels rounding the corner. I stopped in front of her house, turned the volume down, jumped out of the truck cab, climbed into the back and coaxed a Push-Up from the freezer. Digging the toes of my sandals into the steep hill that led to her home, I approached the woman cautiously, knowing that blacks didn't always trust whites.

"How you doin' today, ma'am?"

Her bucket hat, coupled with a toothless grin, made the lady look about as old as the temperature was high. A walking cane crooked around the arm of her rocker. "Oh, not too bad. But this heat . . . "

"Well, you look to me like you need a Push-Up," I said, handing her the treat.

"A Push-Up? Lawd, I love 'em." She peeled the circle of paper off the top and thrust the orangey goodness up the tube. "I be thanking you."

"Oh, you're welcome. My daddy would've said, 'If hell's any hotter than this, I don't believe I can stand it'!"

She raked her upper lip over the sherbet and smacked. "I used to know a white man who said that."

Seeing the open door, I walked through. "I'm Janet Sheppard. And you are?"

She wiped her mouth with her forearm and offered her hand. "Oh, I'm Mamie Johnson. Pleased to meet you." Pausing just a second, she asked, "Sheppard? You ain't blood to the inshorance man, is you?"

"Yes'm, he was my daddy."

Well, I might as well have said I was kin to JFK. Miss Mamie twisted around, grabbed her cane, beat it against the screen door and yelled, "John! Henry! Get yourselves on out here and buy a Popsicle from this girl. Dis here's de Good Sheppard's daughter!"

Telling all her friends to buy ice cream from me, Miss Mamie turned around my failing business. With her encouragement, I traveled Daddy's route, making allies in every neighborhood, selling so much ice cream that some days required restocking my freezer.

That summer taught me many things. What I recall most is that an ordinary man just might leave his children the best legacy after all—the ability to make friends, to recognize opportunity and embrace it with both arms and to live simply, yet happily. Daddy was never rich, but never hungry. He shared what he had. He lived gratefully, modestly and contentedly. He didn't tell me how to live; he lived, and I learned.

Janet in earlier times—with her storied training in karate, she can do anything she sets her mind to!

I Worked Hard for the Money

by
Francine Baldwin-Billingslea

I sat at my desk, with a big adding machine and stack of papers in front of me, feeling disgusted, aggravated and broke. I was thinking about my title of junior biller. Sure, it sounded nice, but my title was nothing more than polite words for "slave" or "flunky" to the senior accountants. I was tired of my boss, tired of my job, tired of the hard work and tired of the sorry, low pay I received every two weeks. By the time I paid my baby sitter, bought groceries and stockings, paid a bill and got clothes out of the cleaners, I was broke. I was thankful my husband had a decent-paying job, but as a young couple, we needed so many things. And the things we wanted, at that point, were just a dream.

One day, I went to my grandmother's house and my cousin was there. She had just started working at a General Motors auto assembly plant and was showing everybody her first paycheck. When I saw it, I couldn't believe my eyes! She brought home more in one week than I brought home in two! She said they were hiring and that she'd bring me an application. I couldn't sleep that night—all I could think about was working at GM and making my dreams a reality.

The next day, when my boss arrogantly dropped *her* stack of work on *my* desk for me and told me to have it in her office no later than 3 P.M., I politely told her I quit. I cleaned out my desk and went home to wait for the auto giant to call me.

A month later, I walked into GM's personnel department and was hired for the second shift. The hours were from 5 P.M. to 2:30 A.M. and sometimes every other Saturday. Overtime was mandatory. I didn't care. At 5-foot 5-inches and just barely hitting 90 pounds, I passed the physical exam and figured they'd give me a job I could handle. Either way, I was determined to earn the money and make my dreams come true.

The man in personnel smiled as he said, "Stand over there with the others. Your foreman will come and take you to the department where you'll be working. Good luck."

I wanted to jump up and down with joy, but I just smiled and said, "Thank you." I walked over and stood with a group of men and one other woman. Finally, a man came, looked at me and whispered something to the man behind the desk, who whispered something back. Then the foreman sternly said to all of us, "Follow me!"

We walked through the loud plant, passing dull-gray unpainted cars on the track. "That's the body shop," he said.

We walked past another area where the cars were nothing but hollow painted shells. Employees feverishly threw carpet, dashboards, radios and other items inside while others jumped in and out of the cars, bolting and screwing things down.

Walking faster, the said, "That's the trim department." Turning a corner, I abruptly stopped and looked up. A car was being lowered from the second level and a young woman was putting something in place for it to gently rest upon.

"What's going on here?" I asked.

The foreman said, "This is the final line. It's my department and where you'll be working." Looking up, he continued. "The guy is working the hoist to lower the car and she's placing the shims it sits on. Come on, you can look on your break."

He crossed over a track. "Be careful, this is the pit," he warned me and the others. I looked down into the faces of grease-covered men as cars slowly rode over them on the tracks.

I followed my new boss to his make-shift office where he handed me a white paper jacket and hat and told me he'd be with me in a minute, after he took the other new employees to their areas. Watching what was going on, I was excited. I had never been in a factory or plant like this before. It was noisy, greasy, dusty and oil was everywhere. Workers shouted, laughed, talked, stared and whistled.

When my boss returned, he told me I was the third woman hired for his department and the first ever to work in the pit! He then took me to the pit and introduced me to my trainer, who told me to jump down and dig in.

I looked down then looked at the trainer. "I'm scared," I said. He helped me down and showed me a heavy, large steel L-shaped air gun. He put a large round bolt in the top of the gun and as a car rolled slowly over us, he stuck it in a hole in the bottom of the car and pressed the trigger. He did this twice, putting two bolts in each car. The trainer then turned to me and said, "Now you try it."

Thinking this looked easy enough, I did as I had been told. But as the bolt tightened securely in place, the gun quickly snapped back and threw me to the floor. Everybody laughed, including my trainer.

As I lay on the floor dazed, embarrassed and covered in dirt, oil and grease, one of the men in the pit said, "You need to have your ass in the kitchen, not in a pit!" Others agreed.

The trainer said, "Try it again." It was an instant replay, happening repeatedly until the man who worked next to me put his hands in my back to brace me. The trainer rolled his eyes and told him to mind his own business.

I found that the cars were going faster than it appeared. Each time I got off the floor and re-situated, another car was rolling over. For three days I was given help, but by the fourth, I was on my own.

Every morning when my shift was over, I went home sore, completely worn out, dirty and covered in grease and oil from head to toe. I'd sit in the tub and soak, almost too tired to wash, and then I'd climb into bed and cry myself to sleep. By the end of the first week, my husband said I smelled like a mechanic and asked me to quit. I promised that I would after we got a washer and dryer and a few dollars in the bank.

By the time I got my first paycheck, I was jumping in the pit and doing my job like an old, but slow, pro. As long as I was braced, I didn't hit the floor. The times that I did, I got up with tears in my eyes, ignored the laughs and comments, dusted myself off and dug in.

The guys laughed and teased. I worked and cried until one day I'd had enough. I threw my gun down, put my dirty, greasy hands on my imaginary hips and told the men where they could go. I told them *I* didn't disrespect *them*, and they were no longer going to disrespect *me*. Like them, I was there working hard and making an honest living, and I said so. I also told them to grow up, and that if they were really men, they needed to start acting like men. When my rant was over, I stood ready to do whatever I had to do and dared somebody to say something. Other than the sounds of air guns doing their jobs, there was silence.

Like shameful little boys, one by one they came to me with their heads down and apologized. They also took down the naked women posters and watched their dirty mouths and conversations. Six weeks later, my foreman took me out of the pit and gave me a better and cleaner job. A young man was placed on my old job, but he quit after three days.

Six months quickly passed and in that time, I bought a new kitchen set, my daughter's bedroom set, a washer and dryer and a car. I had promised I'd quit, but I didn't.

For years, I tripped and fell as I ran up and down the assembly lines, putting in air filters and air conditioning units and installing fenders and electrical harnesses. I installed radiators, drove cars off the line and worked in spray booths, just to name a few of the many jobs I did. I worked on the final line, in the trim department and in the paint department. I used every size air gun there was, and I bolted and screwed down parts I never knew a car or truck had. I worked under, over, on the sides of vehicles and both inside and out. I cried, threatened to quit and begged to be taken off jobs, often in vain and in between the blood, sweat, tears, aches and pains. I worked more long days and taxing hours than not. In order to stay with and retire from GM, I worked in three different plants in three different states. I still don't know how a timid, petrified, 22-year-old, 90-pound woman made it in an auto assembly plant to become a fearless, 130-pound, 52-year-old retired autoworker 30 years later.

We used to say that we made cars and trucks faster than you were allowed to drive them on the expressway. Quality, not quantity, was our motto. Quality is what we gave, and quality is what the company got. We were paid well, had excellent benefits and perks, and our work was done with confidence and pride.

I will never forget the women who, much like myself, integrated the previously male-dominated auto plants and forever changed women's traditional employment roles, receiving the same jobs, pay and respect as their male co-workers. We *all* worked hard for the money.

Can You Hear Me Now?

by
Nona Perry

Upon graduating from high school, I was eager and excited as I traveled to Portland, Oregon, to begin my new life in the workforce as an adult. My only job experience was working at the local theater's concessions stand Friday and Saturday evenings during my senior year in high school. It had been the perfect job for a teenager because it didn't require getting up early to go to work. There had also been an extra perk—my friend, who had a car, worked there the same nights as I did, so off we would go to the armory after work for live music and dancing until midnight. Oh, what fun we had dancing to good local bands and sometimes to great music provided by Paul Revere and the Raiders, The Turtles and Freddy Cannon.

I packed my bags, bought a bus ticket out of Payette, Idaho, and headed for the big city of Portland. As I started my job search, I was determined to prove to my mother that I was responsible. After two weeks and with the help of my wonderful brother and his patient wife—who lived there and were busy raising their energetic four-year-old twins—I found a wonderful studio apartment in downtown Portland. It was in a boarding house for ladies only and was within walking distance of my first full-time job of filing credit reports for a credit bureau. I had become an official tax-paying citizen. I loved walking past all the beautiful tall buildings each day on my way to and from work.

Within four months, the credit bureau promoted me to making phone calls to businesses to obtain new credit information. It didn't take me long to let my mother know about my promotion, and she was happy for me and proud of me for being responsible.

I also enjoyed my new freedom to stay up as late as I wanted. Living in a boarding house full of girls meant there were always guys around and parties to attend. I often joined friends for music and dancing wherever the latest party was happening. The parties often lasted into the night, and flavored vodka was available for those who "didn't drink." These gatherings usually happened on a Friday or Saturday night. But occasionally, there would be a party on a weeknight and, of course, I wouldn't want to miss it. I would go and later pay the price by dragging myself out of bed at 7 A.M. to get ready for work.

The morning after an exceptionally fun and late weeknight at a friend's apartment, and not getting to bed until 3 A.M., I was so not wanting to go to work. Maybe I'd had too much of that flavored vodka the night before. Being tired was not a good excuse to miss work, but I did not want to have a bad attendance record, so off I went, trying to appear bright-eyed and bushy-tailed. The walk to work refreshed me and I felt ready to tackle the day . . . or so I thought.

I arrived at work on time, but that walk didn't work as well as I had expected. The girls in my department guessed I wasn't quite with it, so I shared my secret about staying out late and about all the fun I'd had. I settled into my routine of making calls, but as the day wore on, my eyelids started to feel as if they were made of bricks. As I waited on the phone for one of my credit reports, I rested my elbow on my desk with my head in my hand. As soon as the person returned to the phone with my requested report and started to speak, my head jerked up. Oops . . . I had actually dozed off while waiting for her! I completed my report then took a quick side-glance over at the girls in the office to see if they had noticed. They had, and as they shook their heads in disbelief, they enjoyed a good laugh at my expense. I was so embarrassed!

I have to do better than this and be more alert, or I'll lose my job, I told myself. I sat up straight in my chair, shook my head awake, and then continued making calls.

My next call was to a finance company. After energetically making my request, I gave the clerk the client information. I patiently waited on hold while she searched. *What's taking her so long?* I continued to wait, but as I began to relax, I could not resist resting my head in my hand.

All of a sudden, I was awakened by a dial tone. *Oh, my gosh! We've been disconnected!*

I immediately called her back, and imagine my surprise when she told me, "I said hello several times but I didn't get a response, so I hung up." I had drifted into dreamland and hadn't even heard her return to the phone.

I probably apologized to her too many times, but I was scared. I had put my job on the line and had embarrassed myself—again!

My face turned red as I heard my coworkers behind me, laughing. It took a long time to live that down at work. It was even longer until I stayed out late on a weeknight. And it was several years before I told my mother how irresponsible I had been.

Nona (left) with Pat Nelson celebrating retirement (Nona never has to worry about reporting to work early again!)

Double Crossed by a Dummy

by
Risa Nye

The notice in the paper said, "Recruiting for the Albany/El Cerrito Fire Department." There followed information about a series of qualifying physical tests to be given at a nearby school. The tests were, among other things, the dummy lift, the ladder climb and the hose pull.

I asked myself, *Why not try out?* This was the mid-1970s and even in the enlightened San Francisco Bay area, there were no women firefighters anywhere. *Perhaps I could be the first.* I talked it over with my husband, and he agreed that it wouldn't hurt to try out. To celebrate my decision, I lifted him off the ground in a firefighter-like bear hug. This was going to be fun.

While it didn't occur to me to seriously train for this, I did try lifting friends and acquaintances . . . with their permission, of course. This was surprisingly easy to do, especially when the person being thrown over my shoulder was

177

a good sport. I figured that the ladder-climbing test would be easy, so I didn't practice that part at all. While I was in reasonably good shape at the time, I did no weight training, squats or stamina building, but I still believed I had the ability to pass at least the first hurdle, which was the dummy lift.

As the day of the test grew closer, I wondered what it would be like to be the only woman in a firehouse. *Will I get a space to myself for changing into my firefighting attire? How will it be to spend all day with the guys?* And most firemen I had seen were in great shape and not bad looking, either. *Will my husband of just a year be jealous when I go off to work every day? Will our relationship survive this potential new living arrangement?* He'd be home alone several nights a week, and I'd be surrounded by buff, hunky and probably single men. It was something to think about. I had some reservations, but I figured that there was no point in going over the pros and cons until I had passed the tests.

Finally, test day arrived. The air was cool and clear on a fog-free early spring morning. I took the bus to the test site, which had been prepared to allow for dummy lifting, ladder climbing and hose pulling. It was laid out like a series of track and field events, but in a large parking lot instead, with various stations set up here and there.

I looked around. There were no other women. The men waiting to try out gave each other sidelong glances and smirked as I signed up. I was not yet 25, stood about 5-feet 3-inches tall and was probably wearing earrings. Who wouldn't have laughed at me? I looked them in the eyes and smiled, thinking there was a remote chance that I wouldn't totally humiliate myself. And there was a moment when I could have feigned confusion—"Oh, this *isn't* the garden show? My mistake!"—and could have made my exit right then, but I let it pass. I wanted to see, just see, if I could make it past the first test.

The way things were organized, each event was a direct elimination—if you failed the first test, you went home. End of story. If you successfully lifted the dummy and carried it the required distance in the time allotted, you moved on to the next test. So picking up that dummy was make or break for me. I felt ready. After all, at a recent party I had carried my sister's 6-foot 4-inch boyfriend several feet across the patio in his backyard.

When they called my name, I stepped over to a sturdy cotton-covered dummy that was sprawled on the ground. He looked like a cousin to the dress dummies I used to drape fabric over in my junior high sewing class. This one did not have as nice a figure—it was devoid of any anatomically-correct features—but it looked like a member of the same family. I remembered how we used to try our A-line dresses with the Peter Pan collars on the class dummy to admire our work. Unlike the dress dummy, however, this one had a head, neck, legs and arms. These appendages would prove to be a critical and fateful difference. I glanced again at this figure that was waiting for me to approach, lift and carry it to the marker on the ground several yards away.

Each testing station had a fireman with a stopwatch, and three of us would lift in the same round. At the signal, we ran to our dummies and bent or squatted down to begin the lift.

My dummy's head and torso easily weighed half a ton and the weight distributed evenly, unlike a real human body. The head was as heavy as the upper body, each arm was full of lead and I could not get enough of a purchase on the dummy to get it to sit up, let alone to lift it off the ground. I moved around to the other side, but could not get a grip there, either. I bent over and tried to wrap my arms around the torso, but the uncooperative dummy did not respond.

By now, the other guys had flung their cotton-covered carcasses over their wide shoulders and were striding toward the finish line. My adrenaline pumped hard, and my body shook at each new attempt to pick up that lifeless hunk of dead weight. Ultimately, I ran out of time. Breathless and frustrated, I pulled away and stood up. I was devastated that I got knocked out of the competition on the first test, but there it was.

The man with the stopwatch mumbled something that sounded like, "Too bad," but by then I was just ready to dust off my knees and head for the exit. I managed to get half a block away before hot tears began to fall.

Since I had arrived on the bus, I now needed to walk several blocks back to the bus stop. But a funny thing happened on my way there. I let my tears run their course, and then I thought about what had just occurred. I had failed in a monumental way in front of a group of men who knew I didn't have a chance. I had gone into the test woefully unprepared, but buoyant with belief in myself. And now, defeated, I faced a long, lonesome bus ride home. *Am I still the same person? Do I still have faith in myself? Could I maybe have picked something a little less public to try and to fail at? What is the lesson here?*

I had a long time to think, and by the time I got home, I had figured out a few things. If I couldn't be a firefighter, I still had plenty of options.

Overall, I had never been a big risk-taker. I usually did what was safe and expected. Whenever I began something new, I took baby steps. Except this one time, when I tried to lift the dummy and run with it—a task I was stupendously unequipped to do. But in fact, it felt quite liberating. I had taken a big chance and tried something different. I discovered that I was terrible at it, and I was OK with that. All I could think about was I could tell this story about myself for the rest of my life and people would always be amazed. "You did that?" they would say. "Wow."

Risa recently got to be a firefighter for a day, a dream come true!

How I Nailed It

by
Joyce Newman Scott

I sat on the couch munching a cup of Skinny Pop Popcorn, my 4 P.M. diet treat, and reading emails. That's when I spotted a message from my longtime agent and friend, Cathy.

"I have submitted you for a McDonald's national commercial, please confirm."

I was thrilled. This was the first big commercial I had seen in a while in my age category (60-something) that was not aimed at incompetence, incontinence or impotence. I'm a working actor who made a living in my 30s doing commercials for companies like Levitz Furniture, Carnival Cruise Line and Popeyes Louisiana Kitchen.

I hadn't had an actual casting in a few months, but I controlled my exuberance. As women age, unfortunately so does their marketing appeal. But I wasn't about to let an implied expiration date stop me from the thing I love most in the world—next to my husband and food, of course—which is acting. There is no pull date on my talent.

Cathy has been my agent for 30 or more years, which is how long I've been in the business. And through the course of far-too-many-to-count submissions, castings, callbacks and a fair share of bookings, we have both learned to jot down the date then try to forget about the job until the client makes its first selection and the actual casting takes place. Rejection in the acting world runs about 90 percent. Obsessing over a casting is fruitless and painful to your ego, although I admit I have obsessed many times myself.

I happily confirmed her email. The next morning, I checked my email and learned the casting director wanted to see me the following day, at 11 A.M., and I was to wear an upscale wardrobe. But the thing that bewildered me was that my character was listed as "The Nail Lady." I had no idea what "The Nail Lady" meant since I didn't usually do hand-modeling jobs.

I called Cathy in a panic. She said, "You are going to be in a large room with LeBron James as the star and a multitude of other people who represent the "best of the best." I had worked with LeBron in a commercial a few years before, but unfortunately I had never actually met him. This was sounding better and better!

Cathy continued, "And your nails should have tiny clubhouse sandwiches painted on them."

I gulped a sip of my coffee. "I'm pretty sure my manicurist can't paint small clubhouse sandwiches. And how do you film a '*best* nail lady'?"

Cathy's voice bore a clipped tone. "The casting director said to come with flashy nails."

My mind went scrambling. "How about if I wear my Saint John black jacket with the rhinestones, fancy black crepe pants and a double set of long pearls? That's classy. And then, maybe before the casting, I can run over to Gables Beauty Supply and buy those bright paste-on nails. Is that flashy enough?"

Cathy snickered and read the rest of the audition aloud. "They are also looking for a flamenco dancer, a beauty queen, a philosopher, a contortionist, an emperor." She fought a giggle. "An Elvis impersonator, a Spanish matador and Aristotle."

"Cathy, there is no way that I am going to book this!"

"You going?"

"Any doubt in your mind? Of course!"

"Bye, darling." She hung up.

"Elegant with flashy nails?" I repeated, very confused.

I couldn't suppress the excitement coursing through my veins, but reminded myself that this commercial, like all commercials, could fall through at the last moment.

I went to my closet and scoured through the mess I kept promising to someday organize. I found my black Saint John sparkly jacket and crepe pants. I also pulled out a set of opera-length pearls from my jewelry chest and hung them on the jacket hanger.

Surveying the outfit, I thought, *Classy and elegant.* Then, just for the hell of it, I phoned my manicurist's shop, asking the receptionist if my manicurist knew how to paint tiny clubhouse sandwiches or hamburgers.

"You want WHAT?!"

I quickly hung up.

Early the next morning, I set my hair in heated rollers and did my makeup, adding more contouring eye shadow for formal eveningwear. I put on my outfit, donned my black sneakers and tossed a pair of flats into my good-luck tote bag to change into later. I appraised myself in the mirror and thought I looked pretty good. Checking my watch, I had two hours to find flashy nails and still make it to the audition on time.

Pulling into the GBS parking lot, I went inside and found a sales girl. Eyeing my outfit, she said, "Someone's celebrating Valentine's Day early."

"I'm an actor on my way to an audition," I shared. "You wouldn't happen to have nail paste-ons with clubhouse sandwiches, would you?"

She pointed to an assorted mix. "We've got stars, vertical symbols, polka dots and some 'I Love You' designs for $12. They stay on for weeks."

I shook my head over the price. "Only need them for a day. How do you put them on?"

She looked at me like I was dimwitted, and then spoke slowly. "Stick them on your finger. File off the excess."

"What if I screw up?" I asked.

"That's why they give you 26 nails for only 10 fingers."

I checked my watch. Time was running out. After making my purchase, I sat on a bench inside the store and struggled with the paste-ons. The sales girl avoided me. I mangled several of the little devils by pulling the paper in the wrong direction. That's when I decided to focus on just getting the sticky buggers off the paper and onto my fingers any way I could. On the way out of the store, I defiantly held up my hands to the sales girl, flashing her my red hearts, polka dots and "I Love You" nails.

"Easy-peasy," I said.

I made it to the audition a half-hour ahead of my call time. Several actors were already sitting in the waiting area. After signing in, I took a seat across from a man in a scientist's white lab coat and next to another in pointy black shoes who was dressed like a matador in a red cape. A man entered dressed like an English poet, wearing a gray turtleneck and sport cap, and he sat across from me.

Just then, the inner door to the casting office opened. A gregarious woman in her 70s—dressed as a fairy godmother and holding a wand—practically floated out. As she opened the main door to leave, she waved her scepter at me. "Break a leg," she said.

I wasn't sure if she meant it, but I didn't have time to respond because my name was called. I got in the line to audition. The matador followed me, as well as the English poet. While the three of us waited our turns to go into the audition room, the matador confessed that he was against killing animals for the simple pleasure of eating meat. I suggested that since we were here to audition for a McDonald's commercial, perhaps it would be best if he stayed in character for the next five minutes. He adjusted his red cape and stomped a black pointy shoe.

Once inside the casting room, I took my place on the large red "X" taped on the floor in front of the camera. The matador positioned himself to my left and the poet took his place to my right. The casting director, Brad, gave us a cue. Brad, who I have known for as long as I have been in the business, is a kind man with a big heart and a sense of humor to match.

Brad instructed us that we were to "slate," which meant to state our name, height and show our profiles. When that was done, he then asked the three of us to do a short improv of our characters.

With the camera aimed at me, I smiled confidently and hammed it up. I held up my nails and displayed them as if they were the most attractive fingers in the universe. I turned to the matador, who ignored me by puffing up his chest and waving his cape. When I turned to the poet, I heard Brad from behind the camera say in an announcer-type voice, "And heeeere's Vanna!"

Without giving it much thought, I picked up Brad's cue and said to the poet, "Would you like me to turn your block?"

Brad let out a robust belly laugh. "That sounds like a good offer," Brad said.

The poet smiled, and then as any actor in his place would do, he took the opportunity to steal camera time by reciting a cheesy limerick he had prepared. We all smiled at the camera for one group shot. Brad thanked us for coming. The poet and the matador left, but I ventured behind the camera and gave Brad a peck on the cheek. I told him how good it was to see him. I wasn't sure there would be another opportunity.

Once in the car, I breathed. Elated and exhilarated, I was exhausted, as well. For all that preparation, I had five seconds on camera. Why did I love this world? What was it about this insane industry that hooked me, caused me to crave another hit of adrenaline, another dopamine rush, desperate for another chance to be in front of the camera?

As I drove down a congested highway, I picked at the paste-on nails, managing to tear them off, leaving behind a tacky, brittle surface. My identity was being stripped away, and I couldn't stand the nakedness.

Am I having a bout of post-dramatic stress disorder? I worried.

Using my Bluetooth, I phoned my manicurist, begging her for an emergency manicure. She agreed to squeeze me in. When she asked me what I wanted, I told her I'd like my usual pale pink. The instant-gratification was going to cost me $20, but it was time to push the McDonald's casting out of my mind. It was time to move on.

That night while watching TV, I saw on the 10 P.M. news that LeBron James had broken his nose while playing for the Miami Heat in a basketball game against Oklahoma. A quick clip showed him lying in a pool of blood. I was flooded by remorse then sudden guilt for thinking of myself at this critical time. Damn, I didn't even like sports, and Miami Heat's hero lay there with a broken nose. I felt terrible for both of us.

Late Friday evening, Cathy called, sounding chipper, to

tell me the good news. I had a callback. I was to go back the next day, Saturday, wearing the same outfit I had worn to the original casting. The commercial was moving forward.

This was the first callback I'd had in a year. My initial impulse was to tell everyone I could think of, but there was no time. Running to my closet, I found my audition bag and counted the unused paste-on nails: four pinky fingers and an assortment of thumbs remained. I then pulled out my Saint John outfit and the pearls and hung them by my bed stand. The rest of that evening, I carefully reapplied what remained of the red polka dots and "I Love You" nails.

I got the part, but was recast as "The Wedding Planner." Vanna was back. And it didn't take clubhouse sandwiches to get me there.

One of Joyce's head-shots

Joyce snapped a photo of her nails the day of the audition.

Awkward Conversations

by
Alyson Herzig

My background is in logistics, which is a fancy way of saying the business of everything from the manufacture of materials through the delivery to the final user. I have worked behind a desk, worn steel-toed shoes walking the warehouse, loaded trucks and managed a private trucking fleet.

Managing the private fleet of delivery trucks provided the most diverse group of people I have ever interacted with. I had 20 very different guys reporting to me. Some had just a few years of experience and others were 30-year veterans. Some were religious. A few were jerks, but most were not.

Initially, these guys had a difficult time accepting me as their boss. I can't say I blamed them. I was younger than most of their kids and had never managed a fleet. But after some time, they realized that I valued their input, listened to their grievances, had their backs whenever needed, found solutions to their issues and was available at 2 A.M. when their trucks broke down on the side of the road.

Good communication helped to forge a bond with the guys that apparently let a few think I wanted to know the personal nuances of their lives that would be better shared with . . . anyone but me!

One of my favorite employees was an older gentleman named Milton. He was getting remarried after being a single man for more than 20 years. He came to me one day to discuss his need for some time off. After our conversation, I was pretty sure I wanted to crawl under my desk.

"Hey boss, you got a sec?"

"Sure, what's up?"

"Well, you know I am getting married soon, right?"

"Yes, congratulations! Very exciting!"

"I need some time off before the wedding."

"OK, you got vacation time coming to you."

"Well, it's not for a vacation—it's for a procedure that my lady needs me to get."

At that point in the conversation, I realized how horribly south it had gone. Panic started to set in. My eyes bulged. My heart raced. My only thought was, *End. This. NOW!* But I was trapped. I might as well have been Super Glued to my chair. There was no escape.

"You see, my man-parts are still all whole. My first wife didn't seem to mind. However, before Mildred and I get married, she is requiring me to get a trimmin'."

Holy shit! I was not prepared for that. There had been no training in business school—or life, for that matter—for the, "Hey, I'm going to get the old pencil sharpened" conversation.

"OK, well I don't need the specifics. Just bring in a note from your doctor."

Dear Lord, seriously?! This is NOT happening. I couldn't even make eye contact with him at that point.

"I am gonna need a week or so off because, at my age, this is gonna be pretty painful. But she insists that if we are gonna have sexual relations, I need to have my manhood circumcised."

I'm pretty sure I'm gonna die. Did I just throw up in my mouth?

"Yes, well . . . just go ahead and do whatever you need to do and put in for medical leave." I waved him off, hoping to end the conversation as quickly as possible.

"I am mighty nervous about this and all, so I appreciate your understanding."

I couldn't end this talk quickly enough. I nodded and mumbled, "Yes, of course, best of luck, and take all the time you need."

Milton exited stage left, leaving me trying to erase the horror of that conversation. It has now been more than 10 years, and it is still as fresh in my mind as if it happened yesterday.

My only hope is that Mildred appreciated the pain that poor man went through, because he needed almost two weeks to recuperate from his trimmin'.

I, however, may never recuperate.

An Extra Special Delivery

by
Stephanie Burk, DVM

In 1897, Dr. Aileen Cust graduated from veterinary college in Great Britain, but authorities refused to grant her a license to practice. The Catholic Church considered the idea of a woman veterinarian practically sacrilegious.

The sole woman student in my first employer's 1956 veterinary school class was frequently chased around the anatomy lab by her male classmates with, to put it delicately, the private parts of a stallion wielded by her male classmates.

My favorite male cousin, who graduated from the same vet school in 1970, remembered his three women classmates mainly for the shortness of their skirts.

"I want to be a veterinarian," I announced to my parents in the mid-1960s, peering at them earnestly over my stuffed-animal patients.

"That's a man's job," I was informed, but 17 years later

when I repeated the statement, they were all for it. Possibly they were relieved that I had abandoned the idea of archeology and shifted to something closer to home, where I could take care of my own growing collection of pets.

When I was admitted to the Ohio State College of Veterinary Medicine in 1984, the novelty of women in veterinary school had pretty much worn off. Nonetheless, some male members of my class felt women shouldn't be vets, and one local DVM even daringly voiced that opinion during an undergraduate pre-vet club meeting, despite the fact that the group was overwhelmingly female. I often wondered if he had a death wish.

After graduation, I worked in a mixed animal practice east of Cincinnati, Ohio. I felt reasonably proficient treating dogs, cats and horses, but spent an inordinate amount of time worrying my way out to farm calls to treat other livestock. Besides avoiding embarrassing faux pas that would identify me as a new graduate—such as losing a thermometer up a steer's rear end—I had to prove my capabilities *despite* being "that girl veterinarian."

My boss and I paid frequent visits to Farmer Dan's dairy farm—more frequently than he paid us, incidentally—to address reproductive problems brought on by poor management practices. Despite our best efforts to educate him, he persisted in doing things his way, keeping far too many underfed cattle on his weedy, wind-swept acreage.

One day when my male boss was out of town, Farmer Dan called to schedule some routine procedures for his cows. I offered to go out. "Well, Cher," he drawled—back then

I had long, decorative curls framing my long, decorative nose—"I know you need the practice, but I'd rather have Larry."

I slammed down the phone, fuming. "I hope he has an emergency and I'm the only one available." As the saying goes, be careful what you wish for. Forty-five minutes later, he called again, and shortly thereafter, I found myself contemplating the black-and-white business end of a Holstein cow that was unable to deliver her calf. I could feel Farmer Dan staring beadily at the back of my head, clearly wondering how much of his time and money I was going to waste.

My patient had evidently decided she was done with labor for the day. She chewed unconcernedly on a wisp of hay, oblivious to the two hind legs protruding from her birth canal. *This doesn't make sense*, I thought to myself. This was no young heifer with a small pelvis; she was a full-grown dairy cow. There was enough space to move furniture around in there, plenty of room to deliver a calf.

I began to sweat. What was I going to be able to do that a dairy farmer with 50 years of experience hadn't already tried? I pulled on and lubricated a shoulder-length plastic glove, slid my hand between the two small, knobby legs and heard an angelic choir tuning up for a rendition of Handel's *Messiah*. I had done the one thing the farmer hadn't thought of—a thorough examination. The cow was trying to deliver twins. Farmer Dan had been pulling on two hind legs, all right . . . but each leg belonged to a different calf.

I located a tiny pelvis and pushed, watching with satisfaction as one leg, along with most of my arm, disappeared back into the cow. I could hear Farmer Dan making noises of disapproval behind me as he watched me undo all his work. Biting my lip to keep from grinning, I guided two legs from the same calf into the birth canal. The cow at this point kindly decided to help, and with a timely contraction from Mom, the calf slithered out easily into my arms.

I helped out calf number two, turned to Farmer Dan, blew a curl out of my eye and said sweetly, "Now, while I'm here, do you want me to treat your other cows?"

Wordlessly, he gestured toward his corral.

The angels, directed by pioneer female vet Dr. Cust and consisting of all my female veterinary predecessors, started the *Halleluiah Chorus.*

Stephanie in 1989, during her mixed animal practice days, tending to a patient

Working Girl

by
Kathleene S. Baker

I had less than 24 hours to prepare. With no idea where to begin, my mind spun like a whirligig. I'd just returned home from an exhausting trip, and with such short notice, panic struck. I had to get a move on.

How am I going to pull this off? I thought to myself. I needed a friend's advice. And no, not advice from a girl-friend—this quest required advice from a male. Sure, I could have asked my husband, if I was a lunatic. He was bound to disapprove, and there was no time for a knock-down, drag-out argument. The clock was ticking.

I called David, longtime friend and hairdresser extraordinaire. Much like a bartender, he's dealt with women from every walk of life throughout his career. I knew he would have answers to my occupational questions on the tip of his tongue. And he did.

Late that following afternoon, with my hubby away from the house, preparations began. I hauled out all the makeup I owned and sat down with a magnifying mirror. As I stared at myself in the mirror, David's advice rang in my ears: "Heavy on the makeup, Kathy! Especially the eyes." So I piled it on, all over my face, from foundation to blush to eye shadow.

Never had I applied so much eye makeup! I envisioned Elizabeth Taylor in her role as Cleopatra—but try as I might, I didn't come close to duplicating the look. However, I did emerge quite colorful. Just to be sure I had the look, I piled on even more mascara until my lashes were heavy, but then I feared my upper lids would sag before the night was over. For the final touch, I brushed glitter across both cheekbones and onto my cleavage. Bending over, I juggled my sparkly boobs into a new push-up bra. I stood up, turned this way and that in front of the mirror. *I look HOT! I really do!*

Then I caught myself—was I really about to do this? Before I could talk myself out of it, I grabbed a dark-brown eyeliner pencil and created a beauty mark below my lip and another, on the other side, above my protruding right breast. Gads, I was a sight to behold. *Instead of attracting attention, I'm going to scare away anyone in his right mind!*

"Big hair! You must have big, messy hair!" David had ordered. So I went for it and spritzed, yanked, spritzed and pulled over and over again. In no time at all, my short hair had become gigantic and appeared to have been styled with a leaf blower.

Next came the attire and I followed David's directions to the letter. I crammed myself into the tightest pair of skinny jeans in my closet, and then slipped into a sexy, lacy, black camisole. I tucked it in and ran a gold and silver belt through the loops on my jeans. Then I stepped into elegant 4-inch spike heels adorned with white lace and silver sequins. If I hadn't found them in a resale shop—brand new, for just a buck—my footwear for the evening would never have made the proper statement.

Holy crap, how the hell am I going to even see the sidewalk from up here? But once somewhat settled in those towering heels, I practiced "the walk," which David insisted was crucial. "Strut. You know, strut like you own the sidewalk."

Those shoes had me 6 feet in the air. Hoping not to fall on my face, I practiced my new strut in front of the mirror. *David said to swing my hips at the same time, too.* Talk about confused! I felt like an awkward toddler taking her first wobbly, uncertain steps, and probably looked like one, too. Or an idiot—most likely, a drunken idiot.

I had no idea hookers went through such agony to prepare for work, only to have clothing removed and makeup smudged. With hair already in disarray, I assumed bed-head hair wasn't a major concern to them.

"Jewelry, tons of jewelry—layers of it!" David had stressed. For the evening ahead, I wasn't about to wear anything except costume baubles. Once duly embellished, it felt like I'd gained 10 extra pounds—which made balancing atop those skyscraper heels even more difficult. I chastised myself. *Will I ever learn a dare can be refused?* Probably not. I had never turned one down in my entire life.

My last task before embarking on this new career was

changing handbags. I finally laughed. That was the one thing David didn't have to coach me on. He'd said any of my monster-sized bags would do, and one with bling was preferable.

I had planned my escape earlier that day. Just as my hubby arrived home, I would back my truck out of the garage. And it worked! He must have been weary, for he barely glanced at me.

Happy I had made a clean escape, I went to meet the girls. But I must admit it felt odd to drive along Dallas' streets in a brilliant, red truck, clad only in my underwear from the waist up. *Have I gone middle-aged crazy . . . or what?*

I arrived at our designated location—the truck stop—to find not even one of my daredevil pals. Suddenly, I decided to hide as best I could in my big, red truck. I wanted to preview the garb of the other ladies-of-the-evening before joining them. Soon they began to pull in and park, but none exited their cars. *Crap! Is everyone going to chicken out at the last minute?*

Secluded behind two 18-wheelers, I made the decision not to budge. A driver on my right winked and grinned as he pulled his truck forward and turned toward the exit. I started to get nervous. *What have I gotten myself into?*

Suddenly, a horn blasted behind me, startling me. I sat in my "come-on-I-wanna-lay-ya" working attire, obviously ready to start my day—er, night—just because my crazy girlfriends had decided the evening would be a good one for a few tricks. And now some perv behind me was already honking to get my attention. *I'll bet he can't wait to see me slip my long legs out of this big red truck. Well, I ain't moving, mister, until I see the other girls.*

Finally, a short fella wearing jeans, cowboy boots and a "What Rhymes with Truck" baseball cap stepped out of his rig and approached me. Nervously, I rolled down my window, just a bit.

"Howdy, ma'am," he said, slightly tipping his hat to me. "Are you with those other gals over there?"

Oh no, I thought. *He must want a threesome! No way! No way in hell!*

"Why?" I asked, barely finding my voice.

"Because one of 'em stopped me on my way into the lot and said to tell you to meet them inside the restaurant." Glancing at my attire, he had the good sense to mind his manners and not make any lewd comments. Grinning, he backed away, saying as he left, "Have a good one, now, ya hear? A *really* good one!"

I looked back at the girls' cars. *Empty! They're empty!* They had slipped into the restaurant without me. That's when I spotted a parking spot in front of the restaurant and pulled forward. Looking around, embarrassed by my appearance and afraid I'd see someone I knew, I quickly jumped out of my truck and strutted my stuff into the restaurant.

As I made my way toward my so-called girlfriends, some fella with a deep, sexy Texas twang let go with, "Hello darling," and blew me a kiss. Wolf-whistles and other comments followed. I must admit it boosted the ego of this not-so-young gal. I stood up straighter and pushed the girls out a little further.

There sat my friends, laughing their asses off. I'd been

told we would all dress as working girls as an early Halloween joke, but it turned out the trick was on me. Not one of them had dressed the part. Yet as we sat there, laughing and visiting, I was the only one who was offered "a job." They were bound to have been jealous. Karma is a bitch, you know.

As we parted ways that night, I realized that come what may, I'd probably never be down and out from a financial standpoint . . . because there's always the night shift!

The Happy Hooker, in the flesh!

All in a
Day's Work

Expect the unexpected.

The Luck of the Irish

by
Jennifer Martin

Most people associate golf with St. Andrews in Scotland, the "home of golf." Not me. I associate it with St. Patrick's Day, a fun holiday that I observe in the spirit of an Irish wannabe.

A few years ago, when I worked as a vice principal in a Sacramento high school, I observed St. Patrick's Day as though my name were "Colleen," even though I'm Italian by descent. I'd show up at school wearing green from head to toe and carrying a tray piled high with green-sprinkled cookies shaped like shamrocks. Twinkling green lights decorated my office, and I pinned green ribbons on any staff members who forgot what day it was. At times, when I was really rambunctious, I'd wear my dumpy-looking leprechaun hat and pass out gold-foiled candy that I had found at the end of the rainbow.

I confessed I'm not Irish, but I'm also not stupid. No way would I ever put myself in a position to be pinched by students just waiting to get even with their disciplinarian for not wearing green. I always prepared for the unexpected on any holiday, and St. Patrick's Day, with costumed characters walking around campus, was always a day of camaraderie and fun. It offered a nice change of pace from my high-pressure job of disciplining angry students and dealing with their even-angrier parents.

One sunny St. Patrick's Day proved to be an exception. It was a beautiful day, and the golf course called to me. Even though I was relatively new to the game, I was hooked. *Do I really want to go to school and referee fights?* I asked myself. Students in green would be pinching others who were not wearing green, and that would surely cause trouble. *How can I pass up such a glorious day on the real green—the golf course? Do I really want to spend the day at school, battling in the trenches?*

The choice was obvious. I called in for a "personal necessity day," which is the faculty's equivalent of playing hooky from school.

Soon I found myself playing golf at the Timbers Creek Golf Course in Roseville, California, where my husband, Bud, and I live. It was a day of exceptional weather, no wind, birds chirping . . . a day of glorious freedom. On the fourth tee, I punched the ball with my Light & Easy seven wood onto the green 95 yards away. The ball took two bounces and started tracking toward the cup.

"Go in the hole! Go in the hole!" Bud shouted at the ball. It disappeared from sight. Two residents, watching from their backyard patio, jumped up and yelled, "We'll be your witnesses!"

Stumped, I quickly asked Bud, "Why do I need witnesses?"

"You just made a hole-in-one! People lie about that, so witnesses are now required to prove it."

Talk about mixed reactions. First, I was stunned as I retrieved the ball from the hole. What a surreal moment . . . doing something that Bud, in all his years of playing, hadn't been able to do. A hole-in-one!

I was beginning to feel special, but reality set in. It had all been a fluke. There was no skill involved. It was merely a random act of kindness bestowed on me by the Irish golf gods on my favorite day of the year.

Suddenly, and without warning, I began to get nervous. *Will people think I'm good at golf?* What a laugh! *Will I be expected to duplicate this feat?* Fat chance! Then school came to mind: *What if the staff finds out I was playing hooky? What kind of dedicated administrator am I to leave the campus on such a rowdy holiday?*

My mind continued to race. *What if people at the bar at Timbers Lodge find out about my hole-in-one?* It'd be bad enough to have to pay the bar bill as tradition demanded, but on St. Patrick's Day, all the tipplers came out of the woodwork. One month's salary would barely cover the tab.

I swore Bud to secrecy and we skipped the bar. Instead, we headed home to fix a traditional dinner of corned beef and cabbage, making sure to add green food coloring to the mashed potatoes and to toast myself with a glass of green beer.

The next day at school, I was in the mailroom when one of the football coaches walked in. "Was that you I read about in the paper this morning?" he asked. "Did you get the hole-in-one?"

Busted!

"Yeah, that was me," I admitted, wondering if Bud had ratted on me to the sports editor of the local paper. Turns out the golf pro at Timbers Lodge had called it in after Bud had secretly gone to the pro shop to buy a souvenir of my achievement, a little flag with the date on it to hang on our golf cart.

"Well, give me five!" the coach roared, giving me a smacking high-five. As the staff poured into the mailroom and later into the faculty lounge, I could hear him relaying my good news, all to cheers and applause. The staff loved it.

I was floored again. No one had berated me for taking the day off. No one had even missed me. Not only had I escaped getting into trouble, but I was the new hero on campus. Somehow, I had been elevated to the status of an athlete among athletes. Of course, I'd never tell them that the next hit after my hole-in-one had dribbled a few miserable feet, barely getting off the tee.

Although my colleagues paid new respect to me as a person of outstanding athletic achievement, I knew better. I knew that all my years of celebrating St. Patrick's Day had finally paid off. The luck of the Irish—at long last—had rubbed off on me.

The Entrepreneur

by
Ernie Witham

Being licensed as a "sole proprietorship" business—and no, I don't fix shoes—means I am my own boss and, I've got to admit, I'm pretty dang good at it. I tend to be fair and impartial, easily forgiving myself when I show up late and turning a blind eye when I nod off in my office chair for an hour or two. My company-sponsored meetings often feature taco chips and beer, and the agenda focuses on timely business problems like how to get coffee stains out of my Ernest Hemingway slipper socks and when's the best time to call for an early afternoon tee time at the golf course. Important expenditures like Cheese Whiz and comic book subscriptions are easily approved by a majority vote of one, and my carefully crafted retirement strategy involves the simple twice-weekly purchase of lottery tickets.

And even though I may not be listed on the Fortune

500—or even the Misfortune 500—I am considered a businessman-in-need and, therefore, privy to the many advantages associated with entrepreneurship. For instance, I get calls occasionally from the crème de la crème of recent college graduates wanting to join my operation.

"Dude, I'm, like, totally into verbs and nouns and stuff, and I designed and printed my own diploma at Kinko's. And when I'm not surfing, I have, like, a ton of ambition."

"Oh man, you had me right up until that ambition thing, but I think we have a personality conflict there."

Another thing that happens quite often as an up-and-coming business owner is that people offer me great deals on stuff like office equipment and company insurance.

"So how many copies a month do you make, Mr. Witham?"

"I dunno. Five?"

"Perfect. The new Canon Millennium will spit those out in less than a second, and you can lease one for only $5,000 a year, plus the mandatory service contract, because with that kind of usage it's bound to break down, of course."

"Of course."

"We also sell employee-compensation packages. Has anyone gotten hurt recently at your office?"

"Well, Sam—my cat—fell asleep on my fax machine and was startled when a fax came in offering me a deal on neon signs and outdoor lighting. But he seems to be feeling better since he repeatedly sprayed the thing for three straight hours until he passed out from dehydration."

"Dehydration, huh? Have you considered implementing an office water cooler program? We have a small-business special—75 gallons a week, only $200, and we give you a free cup."

Having my name repeatedly sold to mailing list specialists means I also get a lot of calls and emails from astute salespeople regarding advertising opportunities.

"Mr. Witham . . . good news. For less than the cost of a new car, we can help you create a 30-minute infomercial for the food channel that will be seen by connoisseurs all over the country. "

"But I'm a writer, not a cook."

"Says here you're into hummus."

"Actually, I'm into humor."

"Oh, heck, we don't have anyone buying that. You'd be much better off with the hummus."

Right.

Anyway, as busy as all this sounds, I do allow time each day to daydream . . . er, that is, to reflect on short-term and long-term plans for increased capital gain. And I have identified several new opportunities that I am actively pursuing.

For instance, I hope very soon to go on the Antiques Roadshow where I expect I'll find out that my vintage blacklight posters are worth thousands of dollars and that the strange water pipe that mysteriously ended up in a box of my old college stuff is actually from the Ming Dynasty.

If that doesn't work out, I plan to be a contestant on *Jeopardy!* on the night the categories include "Simple Sports Questions Even a Five-Year-Old Would Know," "Fictional Characters From Books I've Actually Read," "Old Jokes," "Corny Puns" and "Potpourri for Dummies."

Finally, wanting to give something back to the industry—and make a huge profit—I plan on writing a best-seller on how to succeed through hard work and endless determination.

Yawn. Now, if you'll excuse me, I have to get back to work. It's only an hour until lunch, and I'm way behind on my nap . . . ah, I mean . . . research.

Quiet! The Entrepreneur is busy dreaming up his next project.

It's How You Play the Game

by
Amy Mullis

Having your child go to a job interview for that first big job is a lot like riding the log flume at the amusement park. Your life ticks by in halting, never-ending jolts as you ascend, craning your neck to look ahead for possible life-altering developments. Before you know it, you crest the hill and race headlong down a steep, watery chute toward something that is undoubtedly going to pool in your seat and make it uncomfortable to sit still. One second your mouth is open from the anticipation, the next, you're wiping your eyes when the ride is over.

Our younger son was begging for better clothes. When you have boys, projectiles and loud weaponry top their shopping lists, not T-shirts in designer colors. In high school, he wouldn't have cared whether he owned a shirt. Now he was sorting through his closet for something without a ninja on the front.

"Here's one," I said, pulling a shroud-like garment from the closet. "It says, 'I only wear black because they don't make anything darker.' "

"Too dressy."

I hung it back in the closet. I thought, *Somewhere there's a girl who will never get the gift of pearls from her husband.*

I held up a tattered piece of black confetti. "How about the Grim Reaper?"

"Too cutesy."

And I thought My Little Ponies were over the top.

One last choice. "How about this?" He scrutinized the logo and raised one eyebrow. "I give up. Who are the Beatles?"

"A group that needs '*Help*'!" As a mom, I'm an honorary member of the Fab Four.

"Mom, I need a shirt with that thing around the neck."

"A seam?"

"No, that thing that shirts with buttons have."

"You mean a collar."

"That's it!"

"You haven't worn a shirt with a collar since your first Christmas. I tied a reindeer around your neck to keep the applesauce from pooling under your chin."

"Thanks a lot, Mom. This year, I'll do that for you."

What can I say? He learned sarcasm from the best.

"Why don't you tell me what's going on," I asked him.

He heaved the kind of dramatic sigh that comes when personal questions are sure to follow. "I have a job interview."

I saw the "Dependent" line on my tax forms flash before

my eyes. "Really? Where?" I asked. He'd made a career of collecting degrees from the local community college. For all I knew, he was about to draw first blood.

"That big place that makes tires."

I guessed aloud what place he was referring to—the international company that had its own cafeteria and helped sponsor all the big events around town.

"That's the one. If I pass the test and interview, they'll pay for me to get my certificate in maintenance, and then I'll work there."

My concerns instantly gave way to the dollar signs dancing in my head.

"Well, why didn't you say so in the first place?" Before you could utter, "New Hire," we hit the mall and snagged an outfit, including shoes without Velcro. When we were done, he looked like *Time* magazine's "Person of the Year." Who would believe that an hour before, his outfit screamed "Pokémon Master!"

Son of the Year aced the test and got the job. He might have a casual sense of style, but he was right on target when it came to making money.

"What do you think was the biggest factor in getting this opportunity?" I asked him over a congratulatory pizza and milkshake dinner. My thoughts went back to the sharp-dressed man shopping trip we had made together.

"Easy. I listed 'Pokémon Master' on my resume."

Antacids on the Menu

by
Pat Nelson

During the five years that I owned a large deli, my favorite meal was antacids. I didn't expect so many surprises when I bought the place that had long been my favorite eatery.

The first hurdle was to meet my employees. They were used to working for an absentee owner, and they didn't even know the place had sold. They were shocked when I walked in and announced that they had a new boss. There was some nervous scrambling to tidy up the kitchen, and one employee was embarrassed when she arrived late. "Hello," I said. "I'm the new owner, and your shift started 15 minutes ago."

I had a lot to learn about running a restaurant. That first day, I watched with curiosity as an employee hauled several loads of food from the refrigerator near the sandwich-prep counter to the walk-in cooler in the back room. "What are you doing?" I asked, incredulous. "Wouldn't it make more sense to leave everything in the refrigerator for tomorrow?"

"No," was the casual reply. "The refrigerator doesn't work. Hasn't for months."

I stuck my hand inside and felt its warm wall. I'd just bought a nonworking piece of equipment! I panicked, thinking to myself, *The health department could come in at any moment and shut us down! Worse yet, a customer could get sick from foods that had been improperly refrigerated!* I ran out the door with those dreadful thoughts in my mind and shopped for a commercial reach-in refrigerator. By morning, a refurbished model was in place and I'd sent the dead one to the dump.

A few days later, after closing time, I stayed to think about what other changes I needed to make. I'd noticed that unfinished wooden shelves lined the walk-in cooler. It was impossible to do a good job of wiping them down, so I'd have to replace them with metal racks. *And OMG! What's that smell? Did that stuff used to be pastrami?* I was afraid to find out, so I tossed it into the garbage can.

I grabbed a soda and sat down to look over the schedule and time sheets. *What?* I'd seen my baker arrive at 7:30 A.M., yet she had written 6:30 as her starting time. *I'll have to watch to see if this error was intentional*, I thought. *If misstating her time is a regular thing, then what? I don't know how to bake! And I've never fired anyone!*

By the end of the week, I knew that the baker was, indeed, cheating on her time. My restaurant was known for its pies, and I couldn't let the customers down. I went home to practice making piecrust. With a *Betty Crocker* cookbook open on my counter, I floured, rolled and tried to form a decent crust. The dough wouldn't hold together.

Just then, my husband walked in the door and said, "You'll never be able to sell that!"

Up to my ears in flour, I wadded the uncooperative mess into a ball and threw it at the wall. He was right. The stuff wouldn't even stick to the wallpaper! I gave up on becoming a baker myself and hired a friend. The baker I had inherited became my first employee casualty. The words, "You're fired," became part of my vocabulary.

Many nights, I stayed long beyond closing time. One night, I decided to make a sandwich for dinner. I reached under the counter and grabbed a bag of bagels from the bread tray. *That's funny. The bag isn't closed.*

On closer inspection, I found that the tie was still on the bag, but that something had chewed a hole in the plastic and had eaten bits from one of the bagels. I suddenly lost my appetite. Instead of fixing a sandwich, I went to the store to buy a mousetrap. While I was there, I picked up a pack of Tums to alleviate the acid churning in my stomach.

Angry at the rodent that had ruined my dinner, I set the trap and stomped upstairs to the office to do paperwork. Suddenly, there was a loud *SNAP!* and a blood-curdling scream. I had caught the little bagel-thief red handed! *Thank God that mouse didn't start shrieking during lunch hour.* There wouldn't have been enough antacids in the world to get me through that.

After I got rid of the rodent, it was a long night of cleaning, disinfecting and throwing away food. I did learn that the crafty culprit had gained access to my restaurant through a hole in the wall behind the oven drawer.

I sealed the bread in plastic containers after that and saw no further sign of mice dining at my sandwich-making counter. Worried that my little rodent might have a family, though, I found some out-of-the-way places to hide bait traps, just in case. All was well until a poisoned mouse died in the wall, causing a foul odor in the ladies' restroom. After cutting several holes in the Sheetrock and getting into acrobatic positions to search inside the walls with a flashlight and a mirror, I found the demised mouse and removed its stiff carcass so it could have a proper burial at the local dump.

Restaurant ownership was full of other problems, too. One day, the bus dropped off a large, unkempt woman with several huge shopping bags. She came in and sat at a table by a window. Having no money, she asked for a cup of hot water. She seemed to enjoy her teatime, adding packet after packet of sugar and creamer to her cup. It was after lunch hour, and she seemed harmless. Because I felt sorry for her, I filled her up with sugary hot water. She acted strange, talking to herself and watching me with eyes that seemed to see both sides of the room at the same time. Someone told me her name was "Crazy Mary." She didn't return for several days, and I forgot about her.

Meanwhile, a tall, skinny woman with waist-length gray hair came in for the first time. I'd watched her walk by several times each day, back and forth, back and forth, always alone and always wearing the same skirt and matching jacket. I waited for her to come to the counter to place her order. Instead, she wove her way between the tables of seated diners and, as they stared in shock, she snatched partially smoked cigarettes from their ashtrays then casually walked out the door. Because I couldn't control everything that might upset the customers at my restaurant, my stress level went through the roof.

As I learned the ropes, one thing after another always had my stomach in knots. One day, there was Crazy Mary again, only 30 minutes before the lunch rush. *Oh no. I hope she gets out of here before we get busy!*

She went into the ladies' room. I had a lot of work to do, but I kept my eyes on that restroom door and watched for her to leave. After about 20 minutes, I thought to myself, *Look out! I'm comin' in!*

Entering the restroom, there was Mary, tugging up her breeches; she had flooded the entire room with water. Soppy toilet tissue covered the floor. Crazy Mary had bathed in toilet water—her *eau de toilette*. She had used the toilet paper and paper towels as washcloths and had plugged the toilet. I yelled at her all the way to the street and told her not ever to come back. Then I grabbed my mop and bucket and did a fast cleanup just before lunch customers began arriving. Sweat dripping off my face, I looked like I, too, had bathed in the toilet.

When I owned that business, there wasn't such a thing as a routine day. One morning before I left home, an employee called from the restaurant. The weather had been awful, with several inches of rain and more on the way. "I went in to clean the bathroom," she squealed, "and there's a huge rat in each toilet in the ladies' room! What should I do?"

I told her the only solution I could think of: "Flush one toilet at a time and pray. If the rat goes down one toilet without getting stuck, you can flush the next."

I waited, not breathing, the phone at my ear. *What if they won't go down?* I worried. I didn't have a backup plan. I popped an antacid. I heard the first flush, second flush, third flush.

"It worked," my employee finally said, relief in her voice.

Those days of restaurant ownership are just a memory, and I can laugh about the events that caused me so much stress. I've learned that when you're in business, things go wrong, things you can't control. I'm still a business owner, and I keep a Costco-sized jar of antacids handy. And whether it's mice in the bagels, customers flooding the bathroom or some other catastrophe, I just call the problems, "Rats in the Toilet." That helps me remember not to stress, because now I know that some problems can just be flushed down the drain.

Banana cream pie hits the floor . . . just another catastrophe at Pat's restaurant.

Pookie

by
Brian C. Hurley, DVM

As a veterinarian and partner at an animal care center, I attempt to instill a sense of pride in our veterinary health-care team. I often discuss with our team the importance of knowing, believing and living our vision, mission and motto on a daily basis:

- Our vision: It is an honor to celebrate and cultivate the pet-family-veterinary bond.
- Our mission: Our mission is to maintain a dedicated, caring and knowledgeable team committed to providing exceptional client service and veterinary health care. We strive toward this excellence through continuing education, technical advances and compassionate care for all pets entrusted to us.
- Our motto: "Come Join Our Family—A Lifetime Relationship"

This never had more of a meaning than it did when I arrived at work one Tuesday in March 2006, following my weekend off. As usual, I arrived at our facility around 8:15 A.M., ready to catch up with the messages and mail that had arrived since my last workday.

I sat down with my coffee from Dunkin' Donuts and began going through the mail stacked on my desk. Two team members came to inform me of an upcoming 9 A.M. appointment. I was surprised to hear the following account from the day before, but was more than prepared to do whatever needed to be done.

Monday had been a typical day on the phones for the receptionists when, in the afternoon, an elderly gentleman called the office to request an appointment for Pookie. He explained that his wife felt their St. Bernard, the patient, was not doing well, and he would appreciate having the doctor take a look at the dog to make his wife feel better. He went on to explain his wife's concerns that the dog had developed some lumps on its head, and the right eye did not look right. The pet had not eaten nor had anything to drink, and it did not move and had not used the bathroom since they had gotten it more than 10 years before.

Following the explanation of all the problems with their beloved pet, the husband quietly explained to the receptionist that the pet in question was not a real pet. Unfortunately, his lovely wife, suffering from Alzheimer's disease, had turned her attention to a stuffed animal that she treated like a living and breathing entity. She truly believed this pet to be seriously ill. As she later described to me, it had a disposition like no other pet she had ever owned in the past. She just wanted her Pookie to get well.

After discussing the phone conversation with others on the team, our receptionist decided to book an appointment for the following day. The husband, feeling slightly embarrassed by his request, was grateful for the compassion shown by the team handling such an unusual request.

At 9 A.M., the owners of the St. Bernard stuffed animal arrived at our animal-care center where their appointment was handled like any other appointment to walk through our door. Once the owners and dog were in the examination room, the technician came to get me. Staff members were a little uncomfortable going into the room with the owners because they didn't know what to do. Therefore, I decided to do the entire exam myself.

I entered and introduced myself to the husband, wife and Pookie. I took a history and recorded all the concerns the wife wished me to explore. I proceeded to perform a thorough physical examination, addressing each problem the wife had listed. We discussed the findings, and I explained to her that she should not worry because her Pookie was doing extremely well and had adapted to the circumstances of not being able to move, eat, drink or use the bathroom. I also explained the lumps were part of the normal conformation of the skull—they were actually the sewn stitches on top of the head.

I went on to tell her I thought Pookie would be fine, but to lessen her anxiety, I told her I would give her pet a nutritional supplement shot that would last six months. She could not thank me enough for my care of Pookie. I went to the back, drew up 12 cc of sterile saline in a syringe then went back to the room and administered the vaccination.

After asking them if there were any other questions, I escorted the husband to the receptionist's desk while his wife comforted the patient. He shook my hand and told my receptionist that I should receive an Academy Award for the care, compassion and tenderness I exhibited toward his wife and Pookie. He asked if he could come back in six months for a recheck or sooner should his wife need me. I told him I would be honored to see them again in the future.

I spend every day of my life healing the ill cat or dog, performing surgery after surgery, and administering preventative care to the healthy pet. For the remainder of my life, I will NEVER forget the greatest moment of my career, the opportunity to comfort and heal the anxiety of one amazing lady who just wanted what was best for her stuffed animal, Pookie. That day, I truly lived the vision, mission and motto of our animal-care center.

The next day, the elderly couple made another emergency appointment and brought Pookie in to see me. The woman told me that she just found out pets were not allowed where they lived, and she was so afraid that Pookie would be taken away from her. She asked me if I would help her find a good home for her dog.

I told her that I had told my daughter about Pookie and that she would love to give Pookie a good home. The woman was relieved and gave the dog to me. I promised to send her some pictures of Pookie with my daughter so she could look at the pictures and see that Pookie was being well cared for.

Shortly after the last visit, the husband brought me a card and informed us that his wife had passed away. He had to leave in a hurry because he did not want us to see him break down. I am proud to be a husband, father, son and veterinarian, but this man, and the love for his wife, has taught me how to be a better human being. I will be forever grateful and can only say thank you from the bottom of my heart.

Dr. Brian with one of his patients

I Finally Saw the Light

by
Ruth Littner

At first, the thought of working for local government was terrifying. I would be in my first 9-to-5 job since before birthing my babies, and I would not be able to run home if, say, I remembered that I had not unplugged the coffee maker or that I needed a particular blouse for the next day and had not turned on the dryer. I liked being home. I liked taking care of chores and errands and wearing blue jeans, T-shirts and comfy shoes every day.

I knew I'd have to ditch my bunny slippers and put on some "F-me" pumps and try hard to fit those pencil skirts that were made for women trim as pencils. But alas, I needed the money and the benefits. So after 20 years of not working outside my home, I took the job.

I reinvented myself. I resigned from being PTA president. I gave back the Girl Scout cookie-mom job. I had my long, unpainted nails manicured. I applied lipstick, eyeliner and mascara, and I got my hair coiffed. Weekly. I shopped for tailored outfits that fit my "freakishly tall" body. (Thank you, daughter of mine, for that comment.) I squished and squashed my broadened feet into V-shaped toe boxes and cursed the fashion industry. But, DAMN—I looked good!

Then I took my confident self to a new level. I had not had any problems speaking publicly, but I lacked a certain polish. I attended LeTip meetings and even researched a Toastmasters group, where I would have to stand up and speak in front of dozens of people, most of whom were financially successful. Thinking about them in their underwear, or naked, did not help put me at ease. But I learned how to shake hands confidently, how to believe in myself and how to carry on a conversation that included small talk—a ridiculous waste of time, in my opinion.

And then I learned the most important lesson in the workforce—when to keep quiet. Keeping my mouth shut when I had something to say was no easy task. But my future boss told me I would frequently be in front of township commissioners who essentially held my career in their hands. And no matter what I wanted to say, I would have to filter it first. Filtering was the hardest thing for me to learn. And, my boss suggested, "In most cases, just shut up."

I was ready. As a public entity in a newly created government job, I was told that on my first day, the newspapers would interview me and run a story. I had to bring my A-game. And I did. I looked like a million bucks. I stood tall (I had no choice!), I met the folks I would be working with and

I made a great impression. I toured the municipal campus with my boss. I met the judge in the courthouse next door and a bunch of police officers in the police station next to my building. A reporter for a local newspaper interviewed the "new me" and wrote a terrific article. Inside, I was still in blue jeans, but outside, I was someone women could admire.

My first day of work was in late January. I was interested in the work I was doing, and I knew the value of making a good impression, so I decided to work well past my 4:30 P.M. quitting time. My office was on the third floor of an old three-story walk-up mansion. It belonged to the ice cream family—the Breyers—and many said there were "old souls" in the building. Mine was the only office on this floor, the rest of which was used for storage of paper documents and old equipment. The peaked roof and low ceilings were inconvenient for a tall person. But at least I could see from the dormer windows the snowy parking lot below.

There was always plenty of hubbub going on downstairs during the day. I could hear it because my office was not far from the servant staircase, the back stairwell that had been used by Mrs. Breyer's help to get to their small living quarters, now my office. The stairs were narrow and steep. The common staircase only went from the first floor up to the second floor, where the family had slept. I kept hearing squeaks and chains jangling from the rooms next door, but I somewhat nervously chalked those up to "old building syndrome," or the house settling—even though it was a century old—or winter noises like the radiator clanging or mice warming themselves. I tried to ignore the noises, but each time I turned toward a particular wall, with my back to the door, I was sure I felt . . . something. In my high heels, I would clog down to the second floor from time to time just to see real people. Because I was high profile, I could not tell my coworkers that I was just plain scared. I had an image to maintain.

By 5:30 P.M., I was at a good stopping point in my work. At the end of my first day, I packed up my briefcase, shut down the computer and put on my winter boots, jacket and scarf. Then I made a huge mistake. I shut off the light in my office.

With the exception of the mice next door, there was no one left in the building. The lights were off on the second floor, so there was no extant light coming upstairs. It was pitch black in the hallway outside of my office. Even the parking lot had low lighting and any glow those lights emitted only cast shadows into the hallway, diminishing my ability to find my way. I needed to get to the top of the staircase to find a light switch that would help me find my way downstairs—if there was one.

I tried feeling my way down the hallway, but that didn't end well. I tripped over rolls of engineering papers, odd chairs and other hazards. I went back to the office to turn on the light. I peered out to try to guess how far it was to the steps, but the office light barely illuminated half the hallway.

I sat down at my desk and cried. My tears spilled onto my designer jacket. I had spent two months between the time I was hired and my first day of work morphing from a sweet housewife, an earth-mother who had spent all my time with my children, into a working woman who was tough and hard and decisive. And I didn't know what to do. The last thing I wanted was for anyone to find out I was not the image I portrayed.

By 6 P.M., I had heard one too many mice. I knew there was no one in the building, but I could hear children's voices. I heard movement. I heard scraping. And I felt exceedingly uncomfortable. Something was in the room with me. I froze. For 10 minutes, I didn't breathe out of my nose, fearing the wind brushing against my nose hairs would make noise. I controlled the breath out of my mouth. And I had to pee badly.

Too many pressing factors finally forced me to be decisive. I called the police station next door and told the officers of my stupid, stupid predicament. At first, they thought I was kidding, but I convinced them to come.

Four officers showed up, bringing five flashlights. They showed me to the steps where the light switch was, and how to get out should the situation ever happen again.

"It won't," I assured them.

They laughed at me for days, cracking jokes.

I kept that job for 10 years, but I never again went to work without an industrial flashlight. And I kept my co-workers in the dark about my fears.

Minding My Own Business

by
Virginia Funk

My husband, who ran a small sales agency in our home province of Ontario, Canada, asked me one day, "How would you like to run a business?"

Mystified, I asked, "What are you talking about?"

"Well, there's a gift shop for sale in the plaza. You know, it's one of my accounts. I see by their invoices that they do a good business."

The plaza owned the business and had hired a manager to run it. After a number of years, the manager's husband was transferred, resulting in the decision by the plaza owners to sell.

"I don't know anything about running a business. What about our kids . . . they're only nine and 11. They still need me."

"They're in school all day," he replied, "and the school is not far from the plaza. They could come to you after school.

I just know we could double the business."

I dismissed his foolish plan, but my husband was an entrepreneur who often came up with some wild ideas. But after he, with his reputation as a formidable salesman, convinced me to give it a try, we spent countless hours designing and planning "our" concept.

A few months later, we found ourselves out of town at the annual gift trade show, buying products for our newly acquired business. That was a learning experience, deciding which vendors to trust, what items would sell and the quantities to order, and then deciding if the items were still a good choice once the cost of shipping was considered.

On our return from the buying show, we faced the gargantuan task of painting walls and setting up shelves. The front of the store had been securely boarded up because the new windows had not yet arrived. Once shelving was in place, we painted and set up the office. Then our first load of merchandise arrived.

One morning, we arrived to find the boards covering the windows smashed in and several boxes of merchandise missing. We had to report the loss of several hundred dollars' worth of merchandise to the police. I already felt depressed, and we hadn't yet opened for business.

My husband had to leave town for his other job, so, along with my brother's help, I had to finish preparing to open the store in just a week. I was desperate, even putting the kids to work. When opening day arrived and we actually began getting customers, I felt better.

After being in business for about a year, a letter arrived

from the Canada Revenue Agency stating we were about to be audited. This agency is the equivalent of the IRS in the United States. "Are these people crazy?" I asked. "There must be some mistake."

When the government auditor arrived to fulfill his duties, I explained that we'd only been open a short time, but he merely shrugged and said our business had been picked at random. Apparently, small businesses and the self-employed who deal strictly in cash are audited more often than the general population. I learned they sometimes go down a list and, unfortunately, our name came up. "That's how it is done," he said.

Handing over our books in a messy, overcrowded office was humiliating. I hadn't got around to the bookkeeping in some time. I was a jack-of-all-trades and had yet to hire a bookkeeper, reasoning that since I had taken bookkeeping in school, I could do it myself to save money.

When the auditor asked to see the T-1 forms, I stared at him blankly. I had absolutely no idea what he was talking about. It turned out they were forms that had to be completed by each of our four employees and kept on file. I vaguely remembered our accountant telling me about the forms, but I was so overwhelmed with work that I had completely forgotten.

The day was long, and I fumbled as I tried to answer the auditor's questions. I realized how much I had yet to learn, especially as he pointed out the things I was doing wrong. He actually threw up his hands in frustration at the end of the day and said, as he picked up his jacket, "You won't be in business very long!"

"I told you," I cried to my husband, "that I know nothing about running a business. That man made me feel like an incompetent fool. What did we get ourselves into?" He calmed me down, and being the optimist that he was, he said it was just a glitch and that the guy was an asshole.

Time moved on, and I was delighted we were doing a good business. Customers told me the store was beautiful.

But dealing with employees tested my patience. Some turned out to be lazy. One inadvertently insulted a customer, and I gave my standard speech that "the customer is always right," even when I knew that was not true. Her customer had bought six taper candles then left the store and came back moments later to complain that the candles were all broken. The poor teenager who worked after school told her we didn't sell broken candles. After calming the irate customer and replacing the candles, at our loss, I explained to my employee that the lady must have dropped the bag but that perhaps they weren't wrapped well enough.

Another customer returned an expensive Henckels kitchen knife, one of the finest forged-steel blades available. The tip was broken off, and it was clearly evident she had tried to pry a lid. The customer said the knife broke when she was cutting only a refrigerated pound of butter. Again, the customer was right.

I had to deal with one woman who did her annual Christmas shoplifting. Police knew her, but she got away with her crime because I didn't have concrete proof. I finally banned her from the store.

And then there was a "lonely," darling old lady who

came in to chat but who turned out to be a kleptomaniac; and the drunk who came in to return his undershorts, an item we didn't carry; and the haughty woman who bought an expensive floral centerpiece and returned it the next day because it was unsuitable. I was told later, by an impeccable source, she'd used the centerpiece at a dinner party and that she was known to wear a newly purchased dress then return it for a refund the next day.

As the years passed, we insisted our kids—a son and a daughter—had to work in the shop after school. We did not want them to be latchkey kids. Thankfully, they were both interested in sports, which kept them busy after school some of the time. They both hated working at our store. They complained that some of the employees felt they were treated with favoritism. They, especially our son, didn't like to dust the stemware and dishes. He thought it was girls' work, so he used any excuse he could think of to run errands, which always took an extraordinary amount of time.

Years later, the kids told me they hadn't realized how much they had learned, lessons that were invaluable later in life.

Although there were enjoyable times, our business had many ups and downs due to the fluctuating economy. We opened a second location in a new mall, and we hung on there for 14 years, but the rents were so high that we finally closed that location. However, we lasted 30 years in the first location, and I often thought I'd like to meet that asshole auditor once again, the one who said we would not be in business very long.

Raining Cats and Hogs

by
Marijo Herndon

A nine-to-five office job never appealed to me. I like change from day to day, and, above all, I need to be creative in my pursuits. That's why owning a hair salon gave me so many years of joy and satisfaction.

There was always something fun happening at the salon. Each day contained an element of surprise, like the time one of my clients brought her pet miniature pig to visit with us while she had her hair colored. The stylists and clients went hog-wild over that unexpected guest. But now, even after several years of retirement, one memory still stands out above all the others.

My first hair salon was located with a few other businesses in a small strip mall. There was a barbershop, an insurance company and a hearing aid store. An apartment was directly above my salon. The building was busy, with lots of traffic.

But there was seldom cat traffic.

A cat named "Heart Attack" lived upstairs with her owners. I'm not sure that was really the cat's name, but that's what the girls in my shop called her after one fateful day. The apartment was in need of updating, specifically in the bathroom, where a leak had rotted the floor. I think Heart Attack spent most of her time there.

A shampoo room in my salon was located directly below the upstairs-apartment's bathroom. One sunny Wednesday afternoon, as I sat at the reception desk talking on the phone with a client and staring absentmindedly into the shampoo room, I saw something fall through the ceiling and land in one of the shampoo sinks. I continued chatting with my client, not processing what I had seen. After many years of inhaling hair color and perm fumes, hallucinating went along with the job. Sounds of screaming and hissing finally made me realize something was wrong, and that I really *had* seen something fall from the ceiling into the shampoo bowl!

One of the employees yelled, "Oh, my gosh! There's a cat in the sink! And it doesn't look happy!" She then screamed some other words that I dare not repeat.

As professionally as possible, I told the client on the phone that I would call her back. I think I said something like, "Holy mother of God, there's a pissed-off cat in the salon, and I don't think she wants her hair done. Let me call you back." I pulled myself together and contacted the upstairs tenant to tell her that we had something she had lost. "Your cat is sitting in one of our sinks, and I don't think she's interested in getting a shampoo."

Nonchalantly, she said, "OK, I'll be down in a second."

What? Is she used to getting this kind of news? I thought to myself, shaking my head in wonder.

While the stylists and I waited for Heart Attack's owner, we tried to appease the kitty so it would not attack us. She arched her back and flapped her tail furiously. Her fur stood on end. "Nice kitty, nice kitty. It's going to be OK," we said to her in a soothing tone, not unlike the tone we've used with unruly clients.

The fur-ball jumped out of the shampoo bowl, darted across the floor then threatened us with her stance. Clients have sometimes thrown hissy fits when they weren't happy with their hair, but this was even more frightening. At least our clients didn't have the ability to leap out of the sink unexpectedly, claws outstretched, and run rampant through the salon like wild animals. There was that one client with the overly bleached hair that came close, but that's another story.

One stylist, who was working on a client's hairpiece that was sitting on the counter in front of her, stayed calm and cool while cat-chaos ensued. "It's OK, Mrs. Delmonaco," she said to the client. "I won't let the cat get near you or your hairpiece." Mrs. Delmonaco's hairpiece resembled a small woodland creature, and we were all afraid the cat might attack it, thinking it was prey.

It was then poor Mrs. Delmonaco became aggravated. She had lived through the Great Depression and World War II and had lost three husbands. Somehow, seeing the cat run around the salon appeared to be just the thing to put her over the edge. It was as if every trauma she had ever gone through hit her at that exact moment because the look in her eyes was the same as that of a rabbit standing in short grass, trying to appear hidden. For Mrs. Delmonaco, time stood still.

Finally, Heart Attack's owner walked in, smiled at us, scooped up her beloved pet and walked out, never saying a word. She was neither embarrassed nor apologetic. She had a big, proud smile on her face, like she might if she were a little crazy, so none of us said anything. We all stopped what we were doing and watched her take the suddenly calm and loving cat through the salon and out the front door.

Mrs. Delmonaco shifted in her chair and regained her usual stoic manner. The stylists all went back to what they were doing—it was again business as usual. I let out a sigh of relief that no one had been injured, and I called the client I had been on the phone with when Heart Attack crashed through the ceiling.

As I locked the salon that night, I felt grateful that I had a job I loved so much, and I said a little prayer that I would not have another Heart Attack at work.

One angry cat!

A Tacky Position

by
Robley Barnes

For many years, I worked as a chemist and technical manager for a large international adhesive company. As such, I had the opportunity to be involved with numerous new concepts in many differing areas of manufacturing for a wide variety of products. It's not as simple as just "pick it and stick it." Different adhesives are suitable for different uses. Most laypersons would be totally amazed at the multitude of adhesive formulations and adhesive uses. A window envelope, for example, requires three different formulations of adhesive. A hardbound book can require as many as four different adhesives. The list goes on.

One of the more interesting new developments came several years ago when carbonated soft drinks—specifically colas—were beginning to be packaged in the new 2-liter PET (plastic) bottles. It took months of design and testing to get the PET process perfected for mass production. Simultaneously, it took several months of machine modifications of the equipment to use in the labeling operation for this new PET container. And then, it took several weeks to manufacture these bottles and to install the labeling machine at the bottler's facility.

Finally, everything was ready for a production run to evaluate the process. But wait. Then someone realized that there was no adhesive for the labeling machine.

Late one afternoon, I got a panic call. That's when the motto on the sign hanging on my laboratory wall got the extreme test. The motto: "The difficult . . . we do now; the impossible . . . may take a couple of hours."

The hot-melt adhesive I recommended ran well on the first day of trials. The bottles initially looked great, and the adhesive machined well. The next day, however, was a disaster. All of the paper labels had split. Only then was I advised that the bottles were being filled with liquid cola at 35 degrees Fahrenheit. Those PET bottles expanded significantly in the summer heat of a Texas warehouse. The paper labels were not designed to expand. Thus, they split.

After several additional agonizing hot-melt adhesive trial recommendations, we found a successful product. It was a permanently tacky product with some elasticity. As the bottles expanded, the adhesive stretched. There was one minor problem, however. The adhesive was pigmented white—because of the application for which it was initially designed. For this project, the white adhesive could not be visible. Once the color pigment was removed, all was well.

After several months of successful labeling, I revealed to the managers at the cola bottling plant what this product's original use was, the primary function for which it had been developed. It had been designed to act as a POSITIONING ADHESIVE FOR FEMININE SANITARY NAPKINS, i.e., it held the napkin to a female's panty to keep it positioned in the proper place. Their astonished reaction was, "Please don't tell our competitors." Telling would have been tacky, so I never told anyone . . . until now.

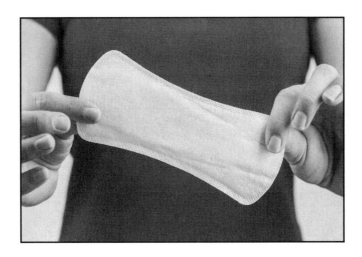

Jobs from Hell

Heaven, help us!

Jewish Coffee?

by
Annette Langer

I'm always up for a challenge. Until the day I checked the postings for job openings, I'd held only clerical-type jobs with the federal government. But I'd spotted an announcement for a federal court reporter position. It sounded like interesting work, and it certainly paid more than what I currently earned, so why not give it a try? How hard could it be, especially since the offering included formal training before taking the final exam? I could *do* this! So I applied for it, took the training, passed the exam and landed the position, discovering that most of my training would occur on the job. Oh well, I wasn't concerned. I'd meet that challenge in due time. It probably meant I'd be assigned to a nurturing mentor who'd help me hone my skills while I earned my paycheck.

I discovered quickly that my new boss was anything but the nurturing mentor I'd hoped for. A short, balding, middle-aged man, the administrative law judge was easily irritated, difficult to please and contrary, at best. If I'd say it's white, he'd say no, it's black. If I'd say up, he'd say down. Every conversation teetered on the edge of debate, and I was never the victor.

He had a short fuse and frequently blustered around the office, slamming down law books on his desk whenever circumstances didn't suit his mood. Once during one of his rants, I almost thought I'd seen him snort clouds of smoke like the angry bull in cartoons. He did everything but paw at the ground before charging.

Chill, mister! I thought. *Uh, I mean, your honor, your highness, your pain-in-the-butt-ness. Life's too short to be stomping around aggravated most of the time.*

But, unfortunately, he never read my thoughts. Still, I'd weigh every word before I spoke to second-guess his "mood du jour" and still frequently ended up saying the wrong thing. The other judges in the office maintained an open-door policy, welcoming interactions with their court reporters. My judge kept his office door closed, and that suited me just fine.

We traveled out of state about every six weeks for the hearings. On our first night out on the road, the judge chose an ethnic restaurant for our dinner. We'd just been seated when he began offering his opinions on such issues as various Civil War battles, the pros and cons of buying stocks on margin and any other subject I had little working knowledge of. I buried my face in the menu, pretending to study it and wishing I'd never have to remove the barrier between us. He stopped talking long enough for the server to take our orders, but then began an entirely new discourse. Like a manic hummingbird flitting from flower to flower, the judge unexpectedly changed topics without warning. I tried to keep up with his tirades, but soon found myself tuning him out as the subject matter became more and more unfamiliar and disconnected.

I'd made it through the salad course without saying the wrong thing and then started on my entrée. I let him drone on with only an occasional "uh-huh" or "mm-hmm" to prove I was still awake. I'd simply nod and chew, avoiding any potentially controversial responses. To buy more time, I picked at my dinner roll, chewing each bit in silence while he continued his oration. *I need more butter!* I shouted in my head. *This bread is sitting like a stone in my throat!*

I knew I'd have to add something to the conversation soon. I felt perspiration forming above my upper lip, not knowing if it was from the heat of the spicy goulash I regretted ordering or if it was just my nerves. I pushed the uneaten food around with my fork, trying to decide whether to mop up some of the gravy with my bread or just leave the chunks of stew alone on my plate to fend for themselves. *I know just how you feel, little goulash. I'm battling a fiery demon, too!*

My mind jumped ahead as I planned possible generic responses to whatever the heck the judge was talking about now. I'm sure my eyes had glazed over about the same time I'd stopped listening to his monologue, probably five or six paragraphs earlier. I hoped he wouldn't notice.

Then I heard him say something about Jewish coffee,

another topic I knew nothing about, and he seemed to be waiting for a reply. *Maybe Jewish coffee is a popular Hebrew term that we Christians weren't privy to, like a secret handshake or something?* But I didn't want to risk it. I knew I couldn't fake trying to guess what he had just said because he'd discover I hadn't been paying attention.

When he stopped to take a swallow of water, I hesitantly asked, "Uh, what *is* that?"

He snapped in his customary impatient tone, "What is *what*?"

"Well," I said, "I've heard of Irish coffee and Mexican coffee, but I don't know what Jewish coffee is. What *is* that?"

Suddenly, it felt as if everyone in the restaurant had stopped their table conversations, put down their knives and forks and leaned forward in expectation to hear his answer.

He paused, exhaled slowly through his nose, looked me straight in the eye and replied in measured tones, "I asked, '*Do you wish* coffee'?"

It still amazes me that I lasted another four years in that job. Challenge met.

Annette finally enjoying a cup of her version of "Jewish coffee."

Summers Digging Graves

by
Timothy Martin

The first car I owned was a 1959 Volkswagen Bug. It had crank windows, vacuum locks and a broken odometer, and it cost a grand total of $200. Every once in a while, someone would ask where I got the money for my car, and I would say, "I earned it digging graves." It never failed to creep them out.

Gravediggers have always given people the willies, thanks in part to Hollywood feeding us a steady diet of horror movies over the years. Many folks are still astonished to discover that gravediggers, or "Excavation Engineers" as they're called today, don't have a thick unibrow, a dragging clubfoot and a bulging hunchback like Igor in *Frankenstein*.

I helped my grandfather, the caretaker at our local cemetery, dig graves back in the 1960s. I started working with him at the age of 12. That may sound young, but those were not touchy-feely times when children were delicately nurtured and tutored. Back then, there were no child-labor laws.

Kids were raised to hold down jobs before they were out of grammar school.

I wasn't frightened by hard work. Nor was I afraid to get my hands dirty. Good thing, because digging graves was both hard and dirty. The tools of the trade were a shovel and a pickax. We dug in all kinds of weather, too—everything from freezing rain to sweltering heat.

But it was steady employment, and once or twice a week someone would die of old age or from an automobile accident and we would grab our shovels and get busy. Sometimes there were dry spells when the elderly thrived and the drunks managed to keep their cars right side up, but that never lasted long. My grandpa and I were rarely out of work.

Grandpa's cemetery duties also included cutting the grass and maintaining the grounds. He would rake the soil over the coffins, clean headstones and plant flowers. Mostly, though, he dug graves. My grandpa was 70 years old but strong for his age. His muscles were lean, and his hands were as tough as wire cutters. He always showed up for work at the cemetery, with the exception of a sick day now and then. Grandpa did a fair amount of "day drinking," and sometimes it got the best of him. On those days, I dug alone.

Without Grandpa's help, it took me twice as long to dig a grave, so I started early. It usually involved about eight solid hours of work. The hole had to be 40 inches wide and approximately 6 feet deep. At first, the job seemed insurmountable. The act of removing a huge pile of earth from the ground, deeper than I was tall, had a somewhat debilitating effect on a 12-year-old kid.

After 2 feet of digging in the black and peaty soil, the many advantages of cremation and the question of why it wasn't a more widely accepted practice filled my mind. At about 3 feet, my thoughts traveled to an exciting baseball game or a cute girl I knew. Sometimes I dreamed about a refreshing swim in the river, anything to take my mind off the monotonous task at hand.

Often, as I dug deeper, I hit rocks, and the work increased in difficulty. That's when I would ask myself many questions: *Why does a grave have to be 6 feet deep? Why not 3 feet, or even 2 feet? Is it because of grave robbers? Or are people afraid a wild animal or maybe a vampire will dig up the dead body?*

Encountering a layer of stone meant the shovel was abandoned, and the pickax was brought into action. I swung it furiously and haphazardly in order to break through the rock. In the ever-deepening hole, it became an instrument of death.

The work continued. On occasion, I would dig a bit off center and encounter the coffin next door. Any uneasiness I might have experienced was instantly erased by the sweat and sheer exhaustion of the backbreaking labor. Besides, the sight of another coffin was an indication that I had dug deep enough. At that point, I was usually elated to see a wooden box, presumably filled with rotting human remains.

Only one thing in the cemetery ever scared me, and that was the vaults. Some families bought large tombs to encase their dearly departed. Everyone from great-grandmother on down was eventually placed in the vault. It made me shiver to think about all those bodies lying around inside dusty chambers and secret rooms, waiting for the right moment to spring back to life and to lurch around the graveyard, zombie-like.

Of course, that never happened. There were no walking dead to frighten me, no banshees, ghouls or otherworldly creatures wandering about. The cemetery was a peaceful place where the deceased came to rest—or to take a dirt nap, as Grandpa liked to say. After I finished my work, I would lean against the cool earth and enjoy a bottle of soda. That was about as exciting as it ever got. But then, in a graveyard you can usually expect your neighbors to be very quiet and completely laid back.

Timothy's grandfather

Out with the Mop Water

by
Stephen Hayes

At the end of my senior year of high school, I landed my first real job. Like many kids raised in sunny California, I'd spent several summers picking pears and apricots, often eating nearly as much as I picked. But this was a real job. I was going to spend my summer as a janitor's assistant at a nearby department store—S. H. Kress & Co.

My best friend Ricky Delgado wasn't impressed when I told him. "I never heard of anyone being a janitor's assistant. What kind of ass-wipe job is that? You mean you're not even going to be a regular janitor?"

I noticed he never burned the pavement looking for a job, yet he always seemed to have spending money. I let his lack of enthusiasm roll off my back and resolved to be the best darn janitor's assistant I could be.

"And why Kress? It's a crummy store." Ricky had been

thrown out of Kress several years back when he was still perfecting his pinching technique, stealing from the store. The manager had promised to press charges if Ricky returned, but that manager had been transferred to another store. A different manager had hired me, so Ricky felt free to return.

I learned on my first day that Mr. Martinez, the janitor, had recently slipped and broken his leg in an unfortunate cleanup mishap on aisle 12. He had a plaster cast on his right leg from ankle to mid-thigh, but he scurried about on crutches so quickly I had a hard time keeping up with him when we toured the store.

Having an assistant wasn't Mr. Martinez's idea. He perceived me as a threat to his job security. His attitude was polite, but he wasn't about to let anyone usurp his prestigious spot as permanent janitor.

The first thing Mr. Martinez asked me to do was clean the ladies' room. "And don't let anyone scream, 'Rape!' when you're in there."

I didn't have any idea what he was talking about and stood there, confused. We were in the back of the storage room, where Mr. Martinez had carved out an office. He grabbed his crutches and off he went to the ladies' room, telling me to follow him.

"First things first," he said on the way there. "You gotta let 'em know you're coming in, so whack on the door good and hard to see if anyone answers. If nobody squawks, yell out, 'Janitor's assistant coming in.' You don't want to bust in when some old lady's doing her business or she'll scream, 'Rape'!"

"Has that ever happened to you?" I asked nervously.

"Nah, but I don't take chances. Follow what I say, and you won't have any trouble. Oh, and always prop the door open with a broom handle so nobody comes in when you're cleaning. Got it?"

I nodded. I certainly didn't want to be accused of rape.

When we reached the ladies' room, I whacked loudly on the door without receiving a response. I yelled, "Janitor coming in!"

"Janitor *assistant*," Mr. Martinez corrected. "There's only one janitor, and I'm it."

"Sorry."

We entered the ladies' room, and I propped open the door with the broom Mr. Martinez had insisted I bring along.

"Your job is to empty the trash cans, clean the mirrors and mop the floors. And do whatever else needs doin'. Think you can handle it?"

I nodded, wondering just how insecure he was to worry about losing a job like this.

All summer, I cleaned the ladies' room, and nobody once screamed, "Rape!" I also had to clean the grease traps under the grill in the lunch counter and change the oil in the deep fryer, two chores that would keep anyone with a delicate constitution from ever eating there.

Ricky came into the store from time to time. I never caught him pinching anything, which was fortunate because Mr. Martinez told me that part of my job was to watch for shoplifters. I worried about having to choose between Ricky and my job, but Ricky remained on his best behavior whenever he visited. Sometimes he'd even help me scrape up the chewing gum kids deposited everywhere.

One day, after emptying the trash and mopping the bathrooms, I headed to the dumpster behind the store. The assistant manager, a friendly young guy who consistently forgot to lock the store at night, asked me to clean up a spill on aisle six.

As I pushed the mop cart over to aisle six, I could hear two ladies talking on another aisle.

"Filthy!" said one.

"They shouldn't be allowed in decent stores. It's horrible," said the other.

I wondered who they were talking about. Vagrants dropped by occasionally, and Mr. Martinez told me to watch out because they had lice and would steal you blind.

When I poked my head around the corner, I saw two white-haired women with vinegar expressions. They were scowling at another woman, who was ignoring them while busily browsing through a display of dishtowels.

The woman on the receiving end of this snootiness wasn't a vagrant, wasn't filthy and she certainly didn't look like she was about to steal anything. She was Helen Delgado, Ricky's mother and the subject of my first real crush.

I'd practically grown up in Helen's kitchen, chattering at her nonstop and pouring out my childish hopes and dreams as she rolled tortilla dough into perfect balls, flattening them between her palms. Helen's laughter was sweet and as soothing as a wind chime. I still had a crush on her.

I was too shocked to speak out, even when one of the old women said something about "stinking Mexicans!" I slowly cleaned up the spill on aisle six without anyone noticing me.

It was the first time I'd witnessed prejudice, and it wounded me deeply since it involved someone so close to my heart. I tried to swallow the lump in my throat then angrily kicked that mop cart to the back of the store. The dirty gray water swirling around the mop spilled onto the floor in several places, but I didn't stop to wipe it up. I couldn't breathe and needed fresh air.

Ignoring the summer heat, I stood beside the dumpster, thinking about those awful women and what they'd said about Helen. My rage went from a simmer to a boil.

Just then, those two old women drove by, using the shortcut behind the store that led to a nearby apartment complex. As they slowly rolled past, I grabbed the bucket off my cart and flung dirty mop water at the open front window of their car.

Had my aim been better, this story would have a more powerful ending, one worthy of Hollywood and the big screen. But, unfortunately, I missed the car completely. Not that it mattered. My act of rage was seen by the store manager who'd chosen that moment to smoke a cigarette behind the store. I was fired, and my promising career as a janitor's assistant came to an abrupt end.

As a kid, the summers I'd spent picking pears and apricots had been backbreaking with low pay, but until I worked at Kress, I'd thought rotten fruit only fell from trees. I had no idea orchards of prejudice could spring up anywhere.

The New Girl

by
Stacey Gustafson

"Is this piece of crap your idea?" asked Bob, one of the sales reps at Computers and More, jabbing his finger into my face. "Are you the new girl?"

Hey, where's my "Hello, pleased to meet you" or "Welcome aboard?" I wondered.

Before I started working at Computers and More, I had the perfect entry-level job at a telephone company. Within three years, I doubled my salary and gained notice by the big guns on the top floor. The brass demanded my expertise for their largest and most complicated spreadsheets and integrated reports. I was the go-to-gal.

One hostile takeover later, goodbye dream job.

After a month's scramble, I clinched another entry-level position with a massive pay reduction at Computers and More, a small computer-reseller company. Ralph, president and CEO, hired me to do sales reporting.

"Are you the new girl?" Bob stamped his foot and stared me down.

Gulp. "Yes, I'm Stacey," I stammered, taking a colossal step back, dodging his spittle. "It's my second day."

"Great. Just great. I guess I'm expected to collect the data for all these reports?"

"Ralph asked me to gather the sales figures for the month from all the reps," I mumbled, looking at the floor. According to my notes, the short, stocky guy in my face was Bob Shackleford, top rep—otherwise known as "La Prima Donna."

"Well, tell him I have a family I never see, and I'm not going to do his stupid report!" he yelled, hands on hips. "Ralph can stick it!" said Bob and with a final flourish, he stomped away in perfectly buffed wingtips.

What the hell was that? I've just been hit by a dinky tornado.

On my first day on the job, CEO Ralph discussed my most important task—preparation of reports to analyze sales figures for the year by territory. For my initial assignment, I collected data from the salesmen, like number of computer units sold and price. I used elaborate spreadsheets like the kind I had created at the phone company. There, I'd dealt with 2,599 sales reps; a measly 12 didn't offer much of a challenge.

After Bob's rant, I walked back to my cubicle and slumped in my chair. *Do I really need this?* I thought. *I can get yelled at anywhere. I'm practically working for free.*

I shuffled through intra-office memos, gathered pads of paper from the filing room, sharpened pencils and warmed up the computer. Then I heard *click-clack, click-clack.*

He's back?

Bob, in his shiny tight suit and tiny loafers, headed straight at me. "Here, take your stupid report," he said, tossing it into my hands. I bent down to catch the last page. "Happy?"

This would not be my last run-in with Bob Shackleford.

I kicked off each morning with coffee-room gossip and a steaming cup of joe, but as I rounded the corner, I detected the bark of an angry pit bull wrestling with a rawhide bone.

"Look at me. Just look at me," Bob roared and clutched the front of his pants with both hands. Covered with wet coffee stains, he ranted, "All I wanted was some stinkin' coffee. Some fool broke the coffee maker, and it spilled all over the place."

"Do you need some help?" I asked, timidly backing away.

"New Girl, get me some paper towels." I stuffed four or five into his outstretched meaty palms and stormed the exit.

"Heard you got hit with Bob's rant," said the office manager at lunchtime. "You're doing a pretty good job handling his outbursts. Keep it up."

Easier said than done.

After two years, my husband announced that we were moving to Atlanta for his job. I submitted my resignation. Thank God.

For my final hurrah at work, I managed some corporate inventory, which included golf shoes and other apparel like gloves, jackets and socks. Sales reps handed these out like candy to customers as small tokens of appreciation, and the reps coveted a few for themselves.

As I restocked the merchandise on my last day, I detected the distinctive *click-clack* down the hallway. "Hey, New Girl, where's my HydroLite tan rain jacket?" Bob asked, nostrils flaring.

"Give me a second," I said, dropping my pen. "Got to go to the storage room to find it." I rushed to collect his items and deposited them onto his desk.

"Thanks, Stacey," he said, without looking up. "Sorry to see you go." Waving his arm in the air, he added, "Heck. Take an extra jacket for your husband. No hard feelings, right?"

"Uh, sure. Whatever, Bob."

As I closed his office door behind me, I rolled my eyes and mumbled to myself, "Yeah, jerk, it's been a *real pleasure* working with you, too."

Sarcasm was the best thing I ever learned from that job.

Stacey (middle) in the reindeer outfit, Computers and More, 1990

Charlie's Angels

by
Debbie Simorte

I once went to work for a man I thought of as "Mr. Mean." It was a job that I got through a temp agency.

A requirement for employment at Mr. Mean's place was to have your photograph taken. One day, I learned the reason for that requirement when Mr. Mean—the company president—left a photo album lying out. It was titled, "Charlie's Angels," and contained a photo of every female employee who had come and gone, complete with degrading comments.

There was a reception desk with an alarm clock stationed dead center. We didn't need a reception desk, because nobody ever came to our offices. The alarm went off every day at 2 P.M. as a warning that Mr. Mean might show up at any time. As soon as he walked in the door, my job was to take his mail to his car and put it exactly where he wanted it—on top of 300 other packets of unopened mail. Then I was to check the gas gauge, and if it read less than 3/4 of a tank, I was to call the service department at his company next door and have them fill the tank.

Mr. Mean never knew my name. He usually had Linda, his assistant, pass his orders along to me. "Find Mr. Mean a mirror for his Navigator that does not say 'Objects In Mirror Are Closer Than They Appear.'" She said these things with a straight face.

One day, Linda sent me to Mr. Mean's office. He said to go to the vending machine next door and to make a list of everything in it. I knew he had already decided what he wanted. "What are you craving, sir?" I asked.

"Just make the list."

When I returned with the list, he pulled a wad of bills from his pocket and told me to bring him two Snickers bars. I tried to get him to keep the money and pay later, but he insisted I carry more than I made in a month to buy just two treats.

I returned with the candy and the wad of money and got instructions to put one of the candy bars in his glove box. I imagined him holding candy bars at different angles to the rear view mirror, studying how close they appeared to be.

After my worrying about carrying all that money, it wasn't money he accused me of taking. Mr. Mean forgot he had told me to put *one* candy bar in the car, and when he couldn't find the second Snickers bar in his office, he accused me of stealing it.

Mr. Mean once called from his bathroom while doing his business because he had seen a magazine ad for a watch he liked. He wanted that watch—today! When he wanted to talk to his wife, even while she was at home with him, he would call and tell us to get her on the phone. If he wanted to speak to his daughter, who ran the company next door, he would do the same thing. He did this because every call he made, even to family, had to be recorded.

Thanksgiving came, and my child became emergency-room ill. Her little neck was swollen wider than my hips, she had a fever and was in pain. After numerous physicians had looked at her, we were sent home with no diagnosis, but told to make sure she had no activity whatsoever until she got treatment Monday, because if this were mono-related, she could "bleed out."

While anxiously waiting for Monday, I called Linda to give her a heads up that I'd be absent. Before the doctor's office opened Monday morning, Linda called to say, "Too bad you won't get paid for the holiday since you're missing the day after. Company rules."

After my daughter's recovery, I wrote a letter to management, enclosing a copy of the rules, along with proof of the medical emergency that had kept me from cataloging candy bars and shopping online for a fool with too much money. It was determined that an error had occurred, and I was promptly paid for the holiday. But suddenly there was a need to change my hours, requiring that I stay in the office until 6 P.M. every Friday, after all of the other staff had left, in case Mr. Mean needed something.

Mr. Mean didn't need anything, but I did. The following Monday morning, I called in DONE, and I joined the other angels in Charlie Mean's album.

Tricks of the Trade

by

Cappy Hall Rearick

I woke up one morning, looked in the mirror and found a divorced woman with no income staring back at me. I needed a plan that would help me find a paying job, and I needed it immediately, if not sooner.

Later that morning, I was seated alone at a Krispy Kreme doughnut shop, furiously writing down job information from the classifieds and munching a chocolate heart-attack-waiting-to-happen. A woman dressed as if she were on her way to an important business meeting—or a funeral—bumped my chair and spilled coffee all over my only silk blouse. While she apologized for the bump, we realized that we had known each other years before when we were in college. That unforeseen coffee spill morphed into the job I badly needed.

Like me, she was an interior decorator. Unlike me, however, she was employed. With dancing eyes, she told me that the woman she worked for was hoping to hire another decorator. Was I interested?

I love it when a plan comes together.

I told my father about the job and the woman for whom I would be working, and he had an old-fashioned conniption fit. How was I supposed to know that my new boss had once been THE boss of the biggest brothel in my hometown? I certainly had no way of knowing that the policeman who arrested her had been my own father. Holy Harlot!

I reasoned that even if she had been intimately involved in the world's oldest profession in the past, anyone with half a brain could see that she was now a legitimate businesswoman who had turned over a new leaf. My parents taught me that everybody—except politicians—deserved a second chance. Hadn't I upended my own domestic status quo in order to snatch a second shot at life? Just saying.

OK, so maybe the first time I met her I was surprised at the mind-boggling amount of fake French décor throughout her home and office. Boss Lady's windows were heavily draped in red velvet and the walls were painted purple and hot pink. She greeted me dressed in a caftan that probably glowed in the dark. A less desperate job applicant might have requested a peek at her professional résumé, but not me. I wanted the job so much that it was easy to ignore my inner voice that was screaming, *Less is more!* I would later learn that *more* was the only word Boss Lady ever recognized.

But I didn't know that then. My focus was on success so that my dad would not disinherit me for working with the prostitute he had once put in the pokey.

I had worked there for a month or so when Boss Lady received a call from a recently divorced man. Will Williamson had purchased a bachelor pad and needed a decorator. Typical of a man enjoying the heck out of his mid-life crisis, he wanted a young decorator with young ideas.

"This is a chance for you to pick up a new client," Boss Lady told me. "Will's got more money than The Donald and he spends it on pretty things. I want you to go over and do what you can for him."

My thoughts while driving to his home that day were centered on nailing a big contract. And if God were not totally pissed at me for ditching small-town domesticity, my dwindling bank account might see a reprieve.

I rehearsed the sales pitch I hoped would keep me off welfare, sucked in my tummy and was about to knock when the door opened. Standing there was a flabby, middle-aged man holding a glass of Champagne and wearing a small Hilton Hotel towel that barely covered Willie's Weenie Wagon. Except for the towel, he was butt naked.

As though he were dressed in the latest fashion trend, he grinned at me, took a sip of bubbly and said, "You're a lot prettier than the last girl she sent over."

That time, there was no way I could ignore my inner voice. It screamed, *Listen up, Dum-dum! Boss Lady doesn't turn over new leaves . . . she turns over new tricks!*

I ran to my car with Towel Man following behind, yelling, "Come back! I want to give you my business!"

Thirty minutes later, I was jobless. Again.

After a week, I landed a job at the department of social

services, and hoped it put my father and me back on speaking terms. My job of typing pink and green identification cards for eight hours a day was the definition of TEDIUM, in capital letters.

I returned to my apartment each day more frustrated and bored than I had been the day before. If I had known then the innate anesthetizing effects in a martini, I would have been hammered before sundown. My inexperience, however, had me sipping herb tea and writing bad poetry.

After a few weeks of whacking out pink and green cards, my supervisor summoned me to his office.

"I've been keeping my eye on you," he said.

Uh-oh. Here we go again.

"You hate this job, don't you?"

I could have said, "Yes sir, Mr. Supervisor, I hate it with a plum-purple passion, but I'm determined to bust through that glass ceiling and pave the way for aspiring women everywhere." As much as I loathed it, I could not afford to lose that mind-numbing job, so I kept my mouth shut.

He cleared his throat. "I realize you're overqualified here. The thing is, I don't have anything else to offer you right now. But I have a friend over at the university who needs an assistant to the editor for a quarterly literary magazine he publishes. My gut tells me that you might be just what he's looking for."

Before my gaping mouth could close, he added, "How about I call him and set something up for you?"

By 6 o'clock that afternoon, I was the new assistant to the editor on a magazine I had never before heard of. For the next few years, the magazine nurtured and honed my basic writing skills until it was time for me to exhume the author buried inside my soul. It looked like I wouldn't have to settle for being an interior decorator for men clad only in towels after all.

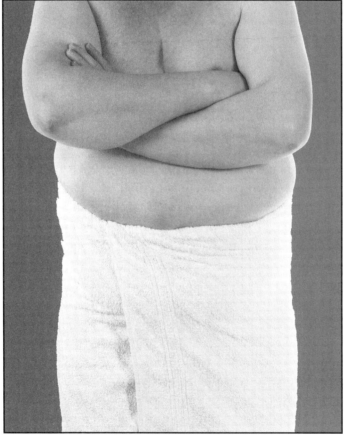

Job loyalty has its limits!

Jobs Not Fit
for Royalty

by

Mary Mendoza

They made a mistake at the hospital when I was born. Instead of sending me home with the Duke and Duchess of Kent, they gave me to an aerospace worker and his schoolteacher wife. Unaware of my royal lineage, the kindly couple raised me as a commoner, hoping one day I'd make them proud by doing what commoners commonly do—getting a job.

Much to my parents' chagrin, I became a Serial Job Seeker.

After graduation, I drifted from one mind-numbing temp job to another. I was a Medicare billing coder (grim); worked in a mailroom dungeon (ghastly); answered phones at an escrow company (utter despair); sold advertising to illiterates (challenging); and at one low point, typed envelopes for eight hours a day for a big company, where I learned how to spell "Czechoslovakia" without looking at my fingers.

I worked for three engineers for four days . . . or it may have been four engineers for three days . . . and quickly locked horns with the babe who ran the office and thought she could run me.

My temp agency extracted me from that fray and sent me to a dentist named Dr. Floss, who, unbeknownst to anyone, had an exceptionally high turnover of receptionists. I was on the job two days when I found out why. Let's just say the DDS found more creative uses for his exam chair than the manufacturer intended. I threw my office key at him and stormed out.

I seemed to attract dysfunctional bosses: the manager who was zonked out on Valium all day and expected me to do her job; the lady embezzler and her charming sidekick; the gal who neglected to mention she was six months pregnant and that I'd be doing her job for half the pay; the crazy publisher with a penchant for parrots; and an eccentric old dame with four incontinent Chihuahuas.

I don't recall how I met the married surgeon, Dr. Sleaze. Suffice to say he was unforgettable, but not in a good way. Besides cutting people up, he was having an affair with one of his patients, a gorgeous Amy Adams look alike.

My job was to juggle his frantic schedule and to lie to his wife about his whereabouts. A balding, unappealing Jewish man, the surgeon looked like Israeli Prime Minister Menachem Begin.

I wonder whatever became of him . . . the philandering doctor, not Begin. Overlooking his moral deficiencies,

I stayed with Dr. Sleaze past my pull date because, I'm ashamed to admit, he was more fascinating than a TV soap opera. Plus, he paid his staff for both Jewish and Christian holidays.

Occasionally, I'd hear about some intriguing job, so I'd fire off one of my captivating cover letters and a doctored résumé, which always got me a callback. One of those brilliant letters snagged me an interview for an editorial assistant position at a magazine. I pictured myself clawing my way to the top of the corporate ladder, becoming the Joan Crawford of the magazine publishing world.

Beautifully coiffed and decked out in a faux Chanel suit, I arrived uncharacteristically on time for my interview with a Mr. Schmuck. When one of my false fingernails snapped off in his hand during the introduction and I tripped on the carpet, I was doomed.

Still hoping for that illusive dream job, I applied for a position in the marketing department of a large daily newspaper. The personnel director—a vicious old crone who hated me on sight—insisted I test on an adding machine, although it was not a job requirement. I couldn't even figure out how to turn the darn thing on. I heard later she hired her niece.

Periodically, I'd have spurts of rebelliousness. I have hung up on a pompous CEO; was nearly arrested at a newspaper for littering; and told the administrator of a prestigious hospital to take a flying leap off the roof because he was annoying the hell out of me. Every time I quit a job in a rage or because I was bored, I'd write a scathing review to the person in charge, outlining my complaints, trashing everyone from the janitor to the vice president, the mailroom minion to the senior editor, thus ensuring I'd never work there again.

Thinking I'd finally put dreadful bosses behind me and was entering a new phase, I was thrilled to be hired as assistant to a TV executive, a thrice-divorced Southern chanteuse named after a dog. It was my second time working for a dog woman, er, I mean a woman with a dog's name. All I can say is this: never work for a woman with a dog's name. It only leads to heartache.

Speaking of canines, during my checkered career, I've been exposed to dozens of "weenie dogs." I'm not referring to frankfurters—I'm referring to the Homo sapiens variety. They're little men, physically and spiritually, with thinning hair, weepy eyes, pale faces, nervous hands and Napoleonic delusions of grandeur.

Never was untreated Weenie Dog Syndrome more evident than in the case of the feckless executive director, the odious toad who fired me from a volunteer job for exposing the unvarnished truth about some office issues. Ever heard of anyone being fired from a *volunteer* job?

One of my most colorful bosses was a glamorous Nicaraguan banana heiress whose family had been driven out of the country by the Sandinistas. She'd built a successful business in the U.S. and needed an assistant. Within a week of signing on, I had convinced her 33 employees that I was Princess Diana's cousin and deserved royal treatment.

I left the heiress for better pay and benefits at an emergency care clinic euphemistically called the "Gun and Knife

Club." The troll in charge was a hillbilly who had risen through the ranks using ruthless Gestapo-like take-no-prisoners tactics, and who delighted in squashing my talents under the heels of her pink pumps.

One horrific day, when I was on my last nerve, a co-worker had the audacity to challenge me about some trivial office matter.

"When I give a command, I want it obeyed!" I barked like General Patton. "If you don't like it, you can stick your head in a fan!"

The troll promoted my co-worker and exiled me to the file room.

In between the heiress and the hillbilly, I found work in a nightclub—no, not as a performer, but as a zookeeper-publicist overseeing a group of adolescent human chimpanzees. It was a constant three-ring-circus that drove me bananas, and, of course, the job ended on a sour note.

After that debacle, I bluffed my way into a job at a newspaper where I lasted two months before being fired for insubordination. That was OK because I was going to quit. I never liked that job, anyway.

Friends and family were shocked when I went to work for a priest. If I could convince the church I was a worthy person, anything was possible. And they had several warnings for me:

"For heaven's sake, watch your language," Mother cautioned.

"Oh, my God," said my husband when he heard the news.

"Merciful saints preserve us!" cried my therapist.

"Somehow I can't see you working at a religious institution," my friend snickered. "Although you sort of look like "The Church Lady" on *Saturday Night Live*."

To no one's surprise, my tenure was brief, my departure dramatic. The priest left the country and the church changed its name, but certainly not because of me.

After my religious experience, casting about for a temp job better suited to my personality, I noticed an ad for a secretary at the local Christmas-wreath factory.

My husband warned me not to apply. "Anyone with a warm body who can type and speak Spanish is highly desirable," he said, "and you will hate the place."

Sure enough, after a five-minute interview, I was hired on the spot. By 9:15 A.M., I knew my husband was right. So at noon, I went home for lunch, called the supervisor and quit. I lasted four hours—a record.

When we moved to a small town, its limited supply of employers made my Serial Job Seeker act trickier. I'm proud to announce that although it took me 15 years, I've managed to offend or aggravate every viable business owner and company in a three-county radius, including my own husband. Yes, the dear fool hired me to be his inept—er, I mean expert—assistant. He fires me on a regular basis, but always rehires me. I think it's because I work cheap.

It wasn't until I was nearing retirement age that I realized the awful truth and halted my insane job quest—I'm unemployable. Anyone as royal as *moi* shouldn't be bossed. *I* should be the boss!

As I relax in my recliner and reflect upon the thousands of soul-sucking job interviews I have endured, and the years I wasted at horrible jobs with horrible bosses, I have only one regret: I wish they'd paid more attention at the hospital the day I was born. Think of it—I could have been the Queen of England!

Mary on a modeling job for a wedding event in 1982.
She said, "I'm no threat to Cindy Crawford!"

Crap!

by
Angela Miranda

I used to be pretty sure I wasn't smart enough to go for a Ph.D. Even so, if I had any hope of getting into veterinary school, I thought a bit of research experience on my resume might help. So I managed to get a little fellowship money and, in the summer before my third undergraduate year, flew to California to spend a summer researching sexually transmitted diseases . . . in cattle.

Yes, cows get STDs. And yes, people study these things.

In case you're a little weirded-out right now, I beg you to bear with me. When is the last time you polished off a hamburger, milkshake or even a sprinkle of cheese—on anything? Ever wonder where all that meat, milk, ice cream and cheese comes from? Or how it happens to be so plentiful?

Most people don't like to think about it, but the truth is that you can't have lots of cheese without lots of cows. In fact, dairy products would not be affordable, let alone widely available, if it weren't for the scientists—veterinarians, researchers and career-minded biology students—who spend their days learning how to make lots of cows.

Making lots of cows means being an expert in cow sex, and that summer, I became part of a research team of such experts. I was to spend my summer looking at organisms under a microscope. Some of the organisms I was designated to study were STD-causing parasites. Others were just microscopic creatures that lived inside cow intestines, making a peaceful living as part of the flora there, not causing disease. Both looked exactly the same under a microscope, causing confusion for cattle producers everywhere.

The easiest place to get a sample of intestinal organisms is—you guessed it—poop. Every week for the whole summer, my job was to go out to a feedlot, put on a long-armed glove and dig around, shoulder deep, inside a bull's rectum. The objective of my experiment was to compare the organisms in the poop to the organisms that cause STDs. This meant that after taking a poop sample each week, my next task was to take samples from the bull's penis.

Cattle are poop machines. A paddy—or sometimes a long, running squirt—gets ejected from a dairy cow's hind end approximately every seven seconds. Don't fact-check me because accuracy doesn't matter here. Once you experience it for yourself, you'll know it feels like every seven seconds. It was during this memorable summer, years before vet school, that I thankfully learned the most essential lesson about working with animals—keep your mouth closed. Most people aren't lucky enough to learn this helpful tidbit until they arrive at their first encounter with a horse in veterinary school.

Except for the diminishing population of farm kids and horse owners who grew up shoveling manure every day after school, the only people down-to-earth enough to deal with this on a daily basis are dairy workers and ranch hands. Lord knows you should whisper a little prayer of thanks to them every time you butter your bread.

But back to the story. My task, upon collecting a sample, was to see how well I could isolate the little organisms from their poop environment. In other words, filter shit. Filter bullshit, to be precise.

This did not turn out to be as easy as it had seemed. We started by putting the poop through a kitchen strainer. After this first pass, we put the poop onto a paper filter attached to a suction hose. Ultimately, our goal was to filter down to where we could see just a single organism, utilizing smaller and smaller filters until we got there. But as it turned out, the manure was thick and fibrous. On a filter, it took on a sort of matted, insoluble quality. Go figure.

We turned up the suction under the filters, but that just made the manure dry out. We were lucky if we got a little liquid out, but it never had enough organisms to survive the isolation process. So there we found ourselves trying to suction palm-sized clumps of shit through micron-sized pores.

And in case you're curious, it just didn't work.

So until I could figure out how to filter these little poop organisms, I desperately needed another way to get more of them that didn't involve suction or filtration. This could mean only one thing—try to make them reproduce. Give them whatever scenario or environment is ideal for reproduction. At this point, all we knew about the poop organisms was that they came from poop and that they looked a lot like STD.

For simplicity, I used to refer to the mystery intestinal organisms as "Fred." In an effort to get Fred to make more Freds, I started putting little tiny drops of poop into every sort of broth we could imagine. Soon enough, placing these tiny samples into the incubator overnight became unpleasant, because every morning as I would open a little packet of sample, a fierce wall of sulfurous, putrid-smelling gas would burst out. It was like the worst fart you've ever smelled. I practiced this ritual with five or six packets of different broth every morning until everyone in the lab, and in the lab next door, and all along the hallway, began to turn away in disgust whenever I came or went. Occasionally, there would be a Fred or two in the broth. But most mornings, it was the odor, not the Fred, which awaited me in the incubator.

I admit I would've done anything possible to avoid another feedlot rectal adventure. But it was time I saw that all the broth in the world was not nurturing my dying Freds. One day, perhaps out of desperation, perhaps out of curiosity, I decided to look back into some of the original poop samples I'd collected weeks earlier. I dipped into the poo that had been sitting in a vial on the counter since my first encounter with a bull's rectum and took a look under the microscope.

Little Freds were everywhere. There were so many of them they were bumping into each other like 8's Euro-trash at a rave, swimming furiously, eagerly and without any direction.

Well, hell, I thought, *maybe the bull's body temperature isn't what Fred likes best. Maybe the incubator, set at a bull's body temperature, normally keeps Fred's population under control.*

After all the trials, I had learned that one thing, and one thing only, made more Freds—poop. At room temperature. Problem solved.

I found out that manure even breaks down and becomes more watery—easier to filter, after sitting at room temperature for a while.

Maybe I shouldn't have tried so hard to make Fred grow in anything other than his favorite place. No matter how much stuff was in the broth that should've been yummy, the little Freds were happiest just swimming and multiplying in five-day-old filth—which, by the way, also smells incredible. Fred just loved poop. He ate it up and proliferated in it at a speed matched only by old-time Catholics, present-day Mormons and all-the-time rabbits.

Perhaps I had wanted to prove something revolutionary, but a good scientist just tests hypotheses until he finds his answer.

Hell, maybe it should have been obvious that turds are unstrainable. But I guess sometimes you try everything first, you go full circle with a hypothesis, you work every angle, everything which, in other circumstances, would seem ideal—until finally you step back and realize that the easiest thing was the best thing all along.

And that is how I learned to filter bullshit.

NYMB Series Founders

Together, Dahlynn and Ken McKowen have 60-plus years of professional writing, editing, publication, marketing and public relations experience. Full-time authors and travel writers, the two have such a large body of freelance work that when they reached more than 2,000 articles, stories and photographs published, they stopped counting. And the McKowens are well-respected ghostwriters, having worked with CEOs and founders of some of the nation's biggest companies. They have even ghostwritten for a former U.S. president and a few California governors and elected officials.

From 1999 to 2009, Ken and Dahlynn were consultants and coauthors for *Chicken Soup for the Soul*, where they collaborated with series founders Jack Canfield and Mark Victor Hansen on several books such as *Chicken Soup for the Entrepreneur's Soul; Chicken Soup for the Soul in Menopause; Chicken Soup for the Fisherman's Soul;* and *Chicken Soup for the Soul: Celebrating Brothers and Sisters.* They also edited and ghost-created many more Chicken titles during their tenure, with Dahlynn reading more than 100,000 story submissions.

For highly acclaimed outdoor publisher Wilderness Press, the McKowens' books include *Best of Oregon and Washington's Mansions, Museums and More; The Wine-Oh! Guide to California's Sierra Foothills* and national award-winning *Best of California's Missions, Mansions and Museums.*

Under the Publishing Syndicate banner, the couple authored and published *Wine Wherever: In California's Mid-Coast & Inland Region*, and are actively researching wineries for *Wine Wherever: In California's Paso Robles Region*, the second book in the Wine Wherever series. They also released *Best of the California Coast* in November 2014; the book features 800 of the best destinations to visit along the Golden State's 1,100 miles of stunning coastline.

Ken and Dahlynn

About Pat Nelson

Pat Nelson was an afterthought, a surprise to her parents, Lee and Ella Hedglin, who already had two teenage sons.

"Patty" was born in Bemidji, Minnesota. There was no hospital in her tiny hometown of Puposky. Her brothers had been delivered at home by Dr. Mary Ghostley, superintendent of the Lake Julia Tuberculosis Sanatorium, where their parents worked.

During her early years, Patty lived on the sanatorium property at the Lake Julia San Dairy, which her father operated. Even though she left Puposky at age four, she never forgot her roots and is writing a book titled *Open Window* about "The San," its patients and its progressive lady doctor.

When she was five, Pat moved with her family to Longview, Washington. She lived there for many years and graduated from R.A. Long High School and Lower Columbia College. Pat is a member of Willamette Writers, Portland, Oregon. She participates in WordFest in Longview, Cedar Creek Writers in Amboy, Washington, and My500Words online. She learned to love the written word and particularly enjoyed creating humor through word play. That is evident in her writing today.

Pat worked for IPCO Federal Credit Union in Longview for several years and wrote the book, *You . . . the Credit Union Member*. She writes columns for *The Valley Bugler*, Longview,

Washington, and has written columns for *The Daily News*, also in Longview. She contributes stories to www.lewisriver.com, an online publication.

Pat's stories have appeared in *Chicken Soup for the Soul* and 10 *Not Your Mother's Book* titles. In addition to this book, she co-created *Not Your Mother's Book . . . On Being a Parent*. She is also co-creating *NYMB . . . On Being a Grandparent* and is currently accepting story submissions for this title. Pat blogs at www.Storystorm.US and is available to speak to groups in her area about the *Not Your Mother's Books* and she presents workshops on writing for anthologies.

Pat lives on a small lake in Woodland, Washington with her husband, Bob, a Great Dane and Labradoodle mix named "Brisa" and a Manx cat named "Peso." She has had careers in credit union marketing, restaurant ownership, and in retail and wholesale, and she now enjoys a career in writing and editing.

Pat reading at WordFest

Contributor Bios

Juli Alexieff is a healthcare professional by day and a maker of stories by night. Her inspiration comes from true-life experience and her yellow Lab—"Lewis T-rubble." She has penned numerous tales of canine antics and aspires to one day be author of her own *Letters to Lewis* series.

Kathleene S. Baker resides in Plano, Texas, with furkids Hank, Samantha and Abby. She has been a columnist and contributor to numerous anthologies and magazines, including the NYMB series and *Chicken Soup for the Soul*. She is co-creator of *NYMB...On Dogs* and the upcoming *NYMB...On Pets*.

Francine Baldwin-Billingslea is published in more than 27 anthologies and magazines including NYMB, *Chicken Soup for the Soul, Whispering Angel, Thin Threads, Silver Boomer, Mused, The Rambler* and *Sasee* and has authored an inspirational memoir titled, *Through It All and Out on the Other Side.*

Robley J. Barnes is a Missourian who has lived in Arizona, Alabama, Kentucky, Tennessee, Louisiana and now Plano, Texas. He is a retired industrial adhesive chemist and a prolific writer of rhymes. A 50-plus year marriage has produced two daughters and four grandchildren. Contact: rbarstar32@hotmail.com

Erin Blubaugh is a teacher and stylist in the San Francisco Bay Area. She is the co-author of *Candidly Speaking: Just Between Us Girls* and a jewelry instructor for Michaels. An avid crafter, Erin blogs about popular products and trends at www.craftfiend.com.

Debra Ayers Brown is a creative nonfiction writer and humor-magazine columnist as well as an award-winning marketing professional, focusing on online and offline branding and sales. Enjoy her stories in other *Not Your Mother's Books, Chicken Soup for the Soul, Guideposts* and more. Visit www.DebraAyersBrown or connect via About.Me/DebraAyersBrown, Twitter: @coastaldeb

Dr. Stephanie Burk—aka "Doc Steph"—is a southwestern Ohio veterinarian who enjoys reading, writing, traveling, gardening and all things equestrian in her not-so-copious spare time. She sounds off occasionally at www.dogphysicsando-therobservations.blogspot.com and hopes to write a blockbuster novel when she grows up.

Barbara Carpenter loves to write and has five books in print with the sixth slated for release in early 2015. Her stories appear in multiple *Not Your Mother's Book* titles and other anthologies, as well as national magazines. She is a quilter, painter and avid grand- and great-grandmother.

Belinda Cohen is a freelance writer and associate reviewer for Every Free Chance LLC. She writes a monthly book club recap and a newsletter at EveryFreeChance.com, offering advice on getting published.

Carol Commons-Brosowske is a native Texan. She's been married 40 years to her husband, Jim. She has three children and is excitedly expecting her first grandchild. She has stories in *Not Your Mothers Books* and *Chicken Soup for the Soul* and she writes a weekly column for *Frank Talk* magazine.

Mona Dawson lives in Northern California in the town where she was born and raised. She loves family, writing, Pacific Grove, wine and everything chocolate, not in that order. Writing for herself, she's been encouraged to share her stories and has two stories in *NYMB...On Family*. Email: ClosedMouth0@yahoo.com

Lola Di Giulio De Maci is a retired teacher whose stories have appeared in numerous anthologies, newspapers, children's books and magazines. She enjoys crossword puzzles, journaling, books, handwritten notes/letters and new beginnings. She writes from her loft overlooking the San Bernardino Mountains. Email: LDeMaci@aol.com

Terri Elders' first anthology submission, "Easter Bloomers," was included by Ken and Dahlynn Mckowen in *Chicken Soup for the Soul: Celebrating Brothers and Sisters*. This is her 100th anthology. Terri co-edited *Not Your Mother's Book...On Travel*. She blogs at http://ATouchOfTarragon.blogspot.com.

Petey Fleischmann was a secretary for 15 years (before computers), requiring her to correct sentence structure, grammar and spelling or to rewrite letters completely. Her style of writing is folksy and she likes GETTING TO THE POINT without using BIG words, making for better and easier reading.

Virginia Funk is retired and has been published four times: *Chicken Soup for the Soul: Finding My Faith; Not Your Mother's Book...On Being a Parent;* and her children's story was published in two different story contests.

Karen Gaebelein enjoys writing about everyday topics to engage her readers and make them laugh. Karen has won honorable mentions from the *Humor Press* and has enjoyed being published in anthologies. Karen can be reached at gabe501@aol.com.

Marcia Gaye, poet and memoirist, writes cross-genre fiction and literary nonfiction. Her career history runs from wrapping pigs' feet in a meat market to editing manuscripts, jobs which are not as dissimilar as they seem. *Times They Were A Changing – Women Remember the '60s & '70s*—includes selections from her upcoming memoir.

Stacey Gustafson is an author, humor columnist and blogger who has experienced the horrors of being trapped inside a pair of SPANX. Her book, *Are You Kidding Me? My Life With an Extremely Loud Family, Bathroom Calamities, and Crazy Relatives* was just released. Website: StaceyGustafson.com, Twitter: @RUKiddingStacey

Stephen Hayes is a Northwest humorist and creator of "The Chubby Chatterbox," a blog focused on humor, culture and travel. Hayes is an artist, traveler and world-class screw-up. His writing is an unabashedly sentimental exploration of growing up in the 1950s, 1960s and beyond.

Patrick Hempfing had a 20-year professional career in banking, accounting and auditing before he became a father at age 44. He is now a full-time husband, stay-at-home dad and author of "moMENts," a self-syndicated column about the joys and challenges of fatherhood. Follow him at patrickhempfing.wordpress.com, Twitter: @PatrickHempfing.

Marijo Herndon's stories appear in several books and publications including NYMB and *Chicken Soup for the Soul*. She lives in New York with her husband, Dave, and two rescue cats—Lucy and Ethel.

Alyson Herzig is the co-creator of the anthology, *Surviving Mental Illness with Humor*, which will be available in 2015.Originally from New Jersey, Alyson now lives in the Midwest, but has kept her sarcastic, cynical Jersey attitude. You can find her blogging about the many disasters and observations of her life at TheShitastrophy.com.

Erika Hoffman writes nonfiction narratives regularly for the *Not Your Mother's Book* series, *Chicken Soup for the Soul* anthologies, *Sasee* magazine of Myrtle Beach and many others.

Fred Hudgin's years of writing poetry have affected how he writes prose. His wife says to put more narrative into the story, but his poetry side keeps trying to pare it down to the emotional bare bones. What he creates is a compromise between the two.

Renee Hughes has stories in the *Not Your Mother's Books...On Dogs* and *On Being a Mom*. She's a CPA, has two grown children and lives with her hubby and rescued rabbit in St. Louis, Missouri. Besides writing, she enjoys acoustic guitar, church activities and indie/alternative music. Website: www.squirrelb8.com

Dr. Brian C. Hurley is a co-owner of the Gardner Animal Care Center in Gardner, Massachusetts. The GACC is a general practice catering to dogs and cats. He became the first veterinarian certified by the American Society of Veterinary Journalists. Visit him at www.GardnerAnimalCareCenter.com. Email: drbhurley@gaccvet.com

Janet Sheppard Kelleher, a humorist, penned *Havin' My Cotton-Pickin' Say,* which describes some of her escapades. *Big C, little ta-ta*, tells how humor helped her cope with—and kick—breast cancer's butt. Her work appears in *Chicken Soup for the Soul*, *The Petigru Review*, *Catfish Stew* and other anthologies. Email: gop53her@gmail.com

Annette Langer writes from Northern California, infusing humor into sometimes-serious topics. Her credits include *Healing through Humor: Change Your Focus, Change Your Life!; A Funny Thing Happened on My Way to the World: Diary of a Fearless Travel Agent* and many shorter works published in several anthologies. Website: www.AnnetteLanger.com

Staci Lawrence is Isla and Shiloh's mommy. She is an ardent producer who co-founded Flash Mob America, the world's first and largest flash mob production company. As an actress and dancer, she has appeared in several plays, TV shows and films. Follow her on Twitter and Instagram @Shugro.

John J. Lesjack lives in Santa Rosa, California, where he is an avid contributor to and collector of *Not Your Mother's Books*. The local junior college creative writing professor and fellow member of the Redwood Writers Club heard John's experience with the balloon plunge and said, "That's an incredible story!"

Ruth Littner, professional editor, is a partner at Gemini Wordsmiths. She penned *Living with Ghosts,* which follows the legacy of the Holocaust through three generations. She contributed to *NYMB...On Being a Woman*. Ruth lives in Pennsylvania with her husband, kids and cats. She loves knitting, volleyball and the Grateful Dead.

Jennifer Martin is a former high school and university instructor, educational administrator, novelist (*The Huna Warrior: The Magic Begins*), award-winning screenwriter and television host/producer. Her critically acclaimed book, *Psoriasis-A Love Story*, published in 2014, is her latest creation. Learn more about her at www.JenniferNMartin.com or at www.HunaWarrior.com.

Timothy Martin is the author of nine screenplays and numerous children's books and is an opinion columnist for the *Times-Standard* (Eureka, California). Email: TMartin@northcoast.com

Frank T Masi edited the nonfiction book *The Typewriter Legend*, published articles in business publications and won poetry awards from the Maitland Public Library. His story, *This is Where I Live*, is included in Florida Writers' Association's short-story collection, *It's A Crime*. Frank is writing a horror-murder mystery.

Patricia Mayes is a retiree from a long career in hospice nursing and now writes with the Cedar Creek Writers, located in North Clark County, Washington State. She also has a busy practice as a grief counselor and spiritual director. Email: patriciajvmayes@gmail.com, website: www.sacredspacespnw.net

Laurel McHargue was raised as "Daughter #4" of five girls in Braintree, Massachusetts, where she lived until heading off to Smith College, followed by the United States Military Academy. Her constant quest for adventure landed her in Leadville, Colorado, where she resides with her husband. Website: www.leadvillelaurel.com

Mary Mendoza is the author of four *Madcap Mary* humor collections (Capralini Press), writes *Udder Nonsense* for *Country Pleasures*, appears in vintage costume at local events and since retiring as an obsessive job seeker, is working on a tell-all memoir. Visit her at MadcapMary.wordpress.com.

Angela Miranda is a veterinarian who writes because she can't shut up when something bothers her. Also, she's hoping for fame and fortune through writing, and this is her first-ever publication. She plans to self-publish the autobiographical *Autistic Stray Dogs*.

Amy Mullis ruins the lives of her children from her home in upper state South Carolina, where she's doing a happy dance because both sons are now gainfully employed. Find Amy's splice of life in *NYMB...On Being a Mom*, the *Huffington Post* and on her blog, "Mind Over Mullis."

Risa Nye is a native Californian. She co-edited *Writin' on Empty* (available through Amazon and Kindle), and published an e-book: *Zero to Sixty in One Year*. She writes essays about creative nonfiction for *Hippocampus Magazine*. Her "Ms. Barstool" cocktail column appears online at www.Berkeleyside.com. Websites: www.EatDrinkFilms.com and www.RisaNye.com

Kim Parsells lives in northern Idaho and tries desperately not to drink and then post things on Facebook that will embarrass her family. She's designed websites for more than 18 years and owns http://SurfIsUp.com. You can reach her at kim@SurfIsUp.com.

Nona Perry recently retired from working at her credit union after 23 years and now enjoys spending more time with her husband and two sweet poodles. She also volunteers for the Rotary and Mobile Meals in Woodland, Washington, and loves housesitting in Kauai.

Cappy Hall Rearick is a 2014 national award-winning syndicated columnist and author of six published books. A popular speaker, she teaches classes in humor writing and memoir. Read her columns, *Puttin' On The Gritz* at go60.us and *Simply Southern* at www.afterfifty.com. For stories and news, go to www.simplysouthern-cappy.com and www.simplycappy.blogspot.com.

Faune Riggin is a program and news director and the host of a conservative radio show. Originally from North Dakota, she has held many pageant titles and speaks on eating disorders. Riggin has two grown sons, two grandsons and a grand-daughter. She lives in Cape Girardeau, Missouri. She LOVES the Dallas Cowboys!

Sioux Roslawski is a third-grade teacher by day, a freelance writer by night and a rescuer of dogs on the weekend. She's proud to belong to the WWWP writing critique group and is thrilled she is no longer a waitress. You can visit her at http://siouxspage.blogspot.com.

Julie Royce, attorney, has published a crime thriller, *PILZ*, and is writing a sequel. She is currently working on a fictionalized biography, *Ardent Spirit,* about Odawa-French fur trader Magdelaine Laframboise. Julie has published two travel books, written magazine articles and is included in several anthologies. Website: www.jkroyce.com.

Stephen Rusiniak is a husband and father from Wayne, New Jersey. A former police detective who specialized and lectured on juvenile/family matters, he now shares his thoughts through his writings and is a proud two-time contributor to the *Not Your Mother's Book* series. Email: stephenrusiniak@yahoo.com or visit www.Facebook.com/StephenPRusiniak.

Joyce Newman Scott worked as a flight attendant while pursuing an acting career. She attended the University of Miami and Florida International University. She has contributed short stories to *Chicken Soup for the Soul* and *Not Your Mother's Books*. Email: jnewmansco@aol.com

Debbie Simorte is a virtual assistant and proofreader by day, works on drafting her first novel by night and wonders why it's so hard to write a short bio. For more silliness, visit her blog, *Writing the Life Chaotic*, at www.writerup.blogspot.com. Email: dsimorte@hotmail.com

Bobby Barbara Smith is a writer and a musician/singer from Bull Shoals, Arkansas. Her humorous, heartfelt short stories have been published in several of the *Not Your Mother's Book* anthologies and in other anthologies and online publications. Bobby blogs at http://indy113.wordpress.com. Website: www.BobbyBarbaraSmith.com

Chris Stansbury resides in northwestern Oregon and is a wife and mother who is semi-retired. Her hobbies are reading, genealogy and quilting. Most of her previous writings have been genealogical histories of family members. This is her first published work.

Don Stewart is the author of *DS Art: The Visual Humor of Don Stewart* (ISBN: 0977329410), featuring drawings from the artist's first 20 years in the studio, and *Past Medical History: Recollections of a Medical Miscreant* (ISBN: 0977329429), a collection of autobiographical short stories.

Camille DeFer Thompson is a freelance writer and blogger. Her short fiction and nonfiction appear in a number of anthologies, including *Not Your Mother's Book...On Home Improvement*. Her feature articles can be found online and in print. Camille lives in Northern California. Visit her humor blog: www.camilledeferthompson.com

Jim Tobalski, after 37 years in management and marketing communications, has uncorked his quirky and humorous outlook by writing just for fun. In his blog www.Mrido.com, Jim parodies his skills as a husband and relationship master. He also speaks about communication skills at conferences, universities and random hardware stores.

Samantha Ducloux Waltz is an award-winning freelance writer in Portland, Oregon. Her personal stories appear in the *Chicken Soup for the Soul* series, numerous other anthologies, The *Christian Science Monitor* and *Redbook*. She has also written fiction and nonfiction under the name "Samellyn Wood." More at http://www.pathsofthought.com.

Clara Wersterfer loves writing, reading stories and playing with her fur babies. She was born and lived in North Carolina then moved to Virginia. She's now a long-time Texan. Most of her stories center on Southern folks, places and events or her beloved animals.

Ernie Witham writes the nationally syndicated column, "Ernie's World," for the *Montecito Journal* in Santa Barbara, California. He is also the author of two humor books and leads humor-writing workshops in several cities. He is on the permanent faculty of the Santa Barbara Writers Conference.

Story Permissions

Slam Dunk © 2014 Juli R. Alexieff
Working Girl © 2014 Kathleene S. Baker
I Worked Hard for the Money © 2014 Francine L. Baldwin-Billingslea
A Tacky Position © 2014 Robley J. Barnes
My First Day © 2012 Erin Blubaugh
Crop Circles © 2014 Debra Ayers Brown
An Extra Special Delivery © 2012 Stephanie A. Burk
Dorothea's Restaurant © 2002 Barbara Carpenter
Read the Label © 2014 Belinda Cohen
Not Everything is Black and White © 2014 Carol Ann Brosowske
Left on the Doorstep © 2014 Mona Dawson
In Memory of Dazzle © 2013 Lola Jean De Maci
Sure Was Greek to Me! © 2014 Theresa J. Elders
Learning to Keep My Mouth Shut © 2014 Phyllis M. Fleischmann
Minding My Own Business © 2014 Virginia M. Funk
What Denomination? © 2013 Karen Gaebelein
Incompetency Takes the Cake © 2014 Marcia S. Gaye
The New Girl © 2014 Stacey Gustafson
Out With the Mop Water © 2013 Stephen F. Hayes
A Job Like No Other © 2014 Patrick L. Hempfing
Raining Cats and Hogs © 2014 Marijo Herndon
Awkward Conversations © 2014 Alyson Herzig
School Daze © 2012 Erika Hoffman
When a KISS is Not a Kiss © 2013 Frederick W. Hudgin
Check, Please © 2014 Renee Hughes
Pookie © 2008 Brian C. Hurley
Following in Daddy's Footsteps © 2012 Janet Sheppard Kelleher
Jewish Coffee? © 2014 Annette Langer
My Tribe © 2012 Staci Lawrence
Learning to Fly High © 2012 John J. Lesjack
I Finally Saw the Light © 2014 Ruth Littner
Luck of the Irish © 2007 Jennifer N. Martin
Summers Digging Graves © 2013 Timothy Martin
A Martini Mishap © 2014 Frank T Masi
What Comes First? © 2014 Patricia Mayes
The Biology Lesson © 2012 Laurel McHargue

A Piece of Cake © 2014 Kenneth McKowen
Jobs Not Fit for Royalty © 2014 Mary F. Mendoza
Crap! © 2012 Angela Miranda
It's How You Play the Game © 2014 Amy A. Mullis
Antacids on the Menu © 2014 Patricia Nelson
Double Crossed by a Dummy © 2012 Risa Nye
What Not to Wear to Work © 2014 Kimberly Kay Parsells
Can You Hear Me Now? © 2014 Nona Lynne Perry
Tricks of the Trade © 2013 Cappy Hall Rearick
Weather Girl Goes Rogue © 2014 Faune Riggin
All's Fair in Love © 2014 Sioux Roslawski
The Unconventional Recruit © 2014 Julie Royce
It Was a Good Place to Work © 2014 Stephen Rusiniak
How I Nailed It © 2014 Joyce Newman Scott
Charlie's Angels © 2009 Deborah L. Simorte
On the Prowl © 2014 Barbara Smith
Losing My Innocence in High School © 2014 Nancy Stansbury
Man of Steel © 2014 Don Stewart
A Slip of the Tongue © 2014 Camille DeFer Thompson
Pole Dancing or Peach Cobbler? © 2014 James Tobalski
Persuasion © 2012 Samantha Ducloux Waltz
A Lunch to Remember © 2014 Clara Wersterfer
The Entrepreneur © 2004 Ernie Witham

Photo Credits

Except as indicated below, the photos in this book were provided by the story contributors and used with their permission.

Cover photo: alphaspirit/Shutterstock.com
Page 99: val lawless/Shutterstock.com
Page 129: Hellen Sergeyeva/Shutterstock
Page 239: Wollertz/Shutterstock.com
Page 241: Nick Barounis/Shutterstock.com
Page 242: Lucas Majercik/Shutterstock.com
Page 269: PeJo/Shutterstock.com

Available Now!

Stand Up! is THE generation-defining book that focuses on the global youth movement. Seventy-five of the world's most dynamic young activists share their amazing experiences and challenge readers through spirited calls to action. By way of their grassroots movements and international work, these young people are bringing their own brand of savvy compassion and unstoppable courage to the crossroads of social enterpreneurship and activism.

Edited and introduced
by John Schlimm

The Cow-Pie Chronicles follows 10-year-old Tim Slinger and his annoying little sister Dana as they grow up on their family dairy farm. Join Tim on his many crazy adventures--from teasing a bull to building forts in the hayloft--and learn about the realities of life on a farm, including the hard work required of Tim and Dana to take care of the land and their farm animals.

Author: James Butler
Illustrator: Lonnie Millsap

Order both from your favorite book retailer today!

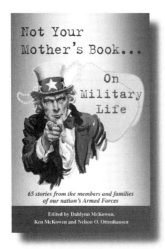

Available Now!

Not Your Mother's Books